The Best Things in Life

PHILOSOPHY IN ACTION

Small Books about Big Ideas

WALTER SINNOTT-ARMSTRONG, SERIES EDITOR

This series publishes short, accessible, lively, and original books by prominent contemporary philosophers. Using the powerful tools of philosophical reasoning, the authors take on our most pressing and difficult questions—from the complex personal choices faced by ordinary individuals in their everyday lives to the major social controversies that define our time. They ultimately show the essential role that philosophy can play in making us think, and think again, about our most fundamental assumptions.

THE BEST THINGS IN LIFE

A Guide to What Really Matters

THOMAS HURKA

OXFORD
UNIVERSITY PRESS

2011

OXFORD
UNIVERSITY PRESS

Oxford University Press, Inc., publishes works that further
Oxford University's objective of excellence
in research, scholarship, and education.

Oxford   New York

Auckland   Cape Town   Dar es Salaam   Hong Kong   Karachi
Kuala Lumpur   Madrid   Melbourne   Mexico City   Nairobi
New Delhi   Shanghai   Taipei   Toronto

With offices in

Argentina   Austria   Brazil   Chile   Czech Republic   France   Greece
Guatemala   Hungary   Italy   Japan   Poland   Portugal   Singapore
South Korea   Switzerland   Thailand   Turkey   Ukraine   Vietnam

Copyright © 2011 by Oxford University Press, Inc.

Published by Oxford University Press, Inc.
198 Madison Avenue, New York, NY 10016

www.oup.com

Oxford is a registered trademark of Oxford University Press

Library of Congress Cataloging-in-Publication Data
Hurka, Thomas, 1952–
The best things in life : a guide to what really matters / by Thomas Hurka.
p. cm. — (Philosophy in action)
ISBN 978-0-19-533142-4
1. Life. I. Title.
BD431.H74   2010
170'.44—dc22
2010009513

1 3 5 7 9 8 6 4 2

Printed in the United States of America
on acid-free paper

CONTENTS

The Best Things in Life

INTRODUCTION

Let's say you're making an important decision. Should you volunteer in Africa for two years after college or go straight into a paying job? Should you stay in a loveless marriage for your children's sake or seek a divorce? Should you take a safe bank job or try to make a living from your music? In each case you can see arguments on both sides, but you want to make the right choice. What is the right choice, and what makes it so?

Your initial questions, about Africa or your marriage, are specific practical ones, about what you should do now. But the last question, about what makes a choice right, is philosophical; it concerns the general standards that should guide any choice in any situation. This book is about that philosophical question, or about an important part of the answer to it.

A complete answer to the question would identify all the factors relevant to a choice and tell you how to weigh them against each other to reach a final judgment about what you should do. These factors would include any effects your choice will have on other people, such as the Africans you'd work with or your children. They would also include any moral duties you have that don't concern effects on other people, such as your duties to keep promises and not to lie. And they would include any effects your choice will have on you and your life. If you go to Africa, you may sacrifice some income, but it will always be true that you spent those years helping others. Will that make your life better or worse? Will staying in your marriage be good for you? Is music better than banking?

This last factor, about the effects of a choice on you, isn't the only one that's relevant and often isn't the most important. (Maybe you'd be better off if you left your marriage, but the harm you'd cause your children makes leaving wrong.) Still, it's always *a* relevant factor, and it's one most of us care a lot about. We want others to live well—we're not totally selfish—but we care rather more about the quality of *our* lives. Even if the same things make anyone's life desirable, we care especially that *our* lives contain them. This is most evident when we make choices that don't involve prior commitments to other people such as a spouse or children— for example, choices about a career. If you're deciding between banking and music, you'll think a lot about what they'd mean for you: you'll want to know which will give you the better life.

Nor is this self-concern always wrong. If you saved two people's lives by sacrificing your own, that would be heroic of you, but it's not something you have a moral duty to do or could be blamed for not doing. While morality requires you to have some concern for other people's good, it allows you to care somewhat more about your own. And most of us do that; in at least many choices we look especially at what they'll mean for us. Abstracting from other considerations, we look at the part of the world that contains our life and ask whether a given choice will make it better, in the sense of containing more of what makes life ultimately desirable.

To do this, however, we have to know what does make life desirable, or ultimately determines a life's quality. Which states or activities improve your life and are therefore worth seeking? Which make it worse? And how do they weigh against each other?

These are the questions this book will tackle, and they're relevant to assessing more than just the effects a choice will have on you. If effects on other people matter too, as they clearly do, it's because they can make *those people's* lives better or worse. If you work in an African village, you may help feed its inhabitants and integrate them a little into the global economy, but you may also partly undermine their traditional culture. Does this combination of effects count in favor of your work or not? The answer depends on whether it makes the villagers' lives on balance better or worse, which in turn depends on what in general makes lives better. To assess any effects a choice will have, you have to know which effects are good and which are bad.

So while our questions don't address everything relevant to making right choices, they do address an important part of it. And they've received very different answers; philosophers have had different views about what things are ultimately good.

One view, held for example by Thomas Hobbes, says the best life you can lead is whichever gives you the most of what you really want; likewise, the best life for another person is what gives her what she wants. Now, it may seem that what you want should be obvious to you, but sometimes our true desires are hidden from us. So you can ask, "Do I really want to work in Africa, or is this just something I think will impress my friends?" "Do I love music enough to run the risk of poverty?" The assumption here is that a choice can be wrong if it doesn't give you what you really want, but the want itself can't be wrong. If you truly desire something, whatever gets it for you is good.

This view seems fine for trivial choices such as what to eat in a restaurant or what movie to see tonight ("Do I feel like watching a romantic comedy or a horror flick?"). But many of us don't think it's appropriate for more important choices. That you most want to be a couch potato doesn't make your living as a couch potato best, especially if you have other talents you could develop; that you care most about the income a job pays doesn't automatically make banking better for you than music. In important choices, such as about your career, what's right isn't determined just by your desires. There are independent standards that make some things better or more worth wanting than others, and the best life is the one that contains the most of those things.

This has certainly been the dominant view in Western philosophy; philosophers have wanted to identify the things that are good independently of our desiring them. But they've differed about what these things are.

Some, such as Epicurus and Jeremy Bentham, believed that the only ultimate good is pleasure. The best life anyone can lead is then the one that feels best; if you're wondering which choice about Africa or your marriage will be best for you, it's the one that will give you the most pleasure. But others have rejected this view. Socrates, Plato, and Aristotle thought the greatest good is knowledge and, more specifically, philosophical discussion or contemplation. That's why Socrates said "the unexamined life is not worth living"—he preferred to die rather than not philosophize. These philosophers believed that a more intellectual life is better even if it's less pleasant. The Stoics and Immanuel Kant, by contrast, thought the only good is moral virtue—neither pleasure nor knowledge has true worth—while Karl Marx equated our good with free creativity, Friedrich Nietzsche with exercising a will to power, and others with religious devotion to God.

These ideas all concern what's good in itself or intrinsically rather than as a means. Many things are good only because they lead to something else that's good. Eating chocolate, for example, is good because it gives you pleasure, but if it didn't—if you got no enjoyment whatever from it—it would be valueless. The same goes for money: it's worth seeking if it'll help you attain other goods but not if it won't. (That's why a miser's love of money is fetishistic: he values for itself what matters only as a means.) Some things are harder to classify. Maybe power over other people is good only instrumentally, or for the other things it can help you get; maybe exercising power and thereby having more impact on the world is desirable in itself. And some things can be good both in themselves and instrumentally; scientific knowledge can be both worth having for itself and useful for achieving other goals. But nothing can be good as a means unless some things are good in themselves. There have to be intrinsic goods that the instrumental goods lead to and from which they derive their worth, and the main philosophical question has been what these ultimate goods are. That's what Epicurus, Socrates, and the others were debating; they were asking what by itself, and apart from any effects, makes our lives worth living.

This is also the question we'll explore in this book, and we'll do so not by reverently studying the opinions of the Great Dead Philosophers as if whatever they said must be true, but by looking at the leading candidates for human value as they appear to us now, in the twenty-first century, and trying ourselves to assess their worth. Does it seem to us now that pleasure is the only good? Are knowledge and creativity good? Does being morally bad make your life worse? The philosophers of the past can help us think about these questions, but we also can and must reflect on them for ourselves.

As we do so, I'll defend two related claims. One is that, contrary to Epicurus, Socrates, and many others, there isn't just one ultimate good—there are many. Pleasure isn't the only good thing in life, nor is philosophical understanding; each is just one item on a longer list of goods, so an ideal life can contain different good things. The second claim is that there isn't a single best human life, say, that of a gourmet or a philosopher, but many kinds of good life. If there are many ultimate goods, then different lives can focus on different ones among them and still be equally good; a life of pleasure can be good, as can one of knowledge or creativity. Moreover, many individual goods can be realized in different ways. Different people can find pleasure in different things, understand different subjects, or achieve things in different domains: in basketball for one, business for another, art for a third. So not only are there many ultimate goods, there can be many ways of achieving a given one.

This doesn't mean we can't compare lives in value, or that all are equally good. Alongside the human goods are evils such as suffering, self-delusion, and moral vice; a life containing only these isn't good at all. And even lives that are predominantly good can be good to different degrees. One can be happier than another or contain more significant achievements; one can be more knowledgeable or combine its elements in a more harmonious way. Sometimes, faced with two possible lives, we can't say that one would be clearly better than the other; the choice between them is a toss-up. But at other times we can see that one life is better and choose it for that reason. To do this, however, we must first have identified the ultimate values or goods in life.

There's no easy way to do this. We can't just extract the goods from science, as if a biology experiment could tell us what they are, or have them delivered to us by religion. We have to think about the candidate goods ourselves, as hard as we can, both in the abstract and as they appear in particular situations. Does it seem right that pleasure is good, both in general and when we think, say, of getting a massage at the end of a stressful day? Is it right that being virtuous—for example, feeling compassion for a friend's pain—is good? Is knowledge good? There's no guarantee we'll all agree about these questions; each has to answer them for herself. But we can work on them together and at least come to a shared understanding of what the main possible answers are.

My discussion will assume that some answers are right and others wrong and that some things are truly good while others are not, so someone's opinion on the matter can be mistaken. Even so, she may have a right to act on her mistaken belief when making choices about her life.

Imagine that music is in fact better than banking, and you know this. But a friend with real musical talent thinks banking is better and has decided to pursue that career instead. You may try to persuade her of music's greater merits, but if you fail, it would surely be wrong of you to try to force her into music. Even if you're correct and she's mistaken, the decision about her career is hers to make. Successfully forcing her into music might make her life better, but given her right to choose her life herself, doing it would be wrong.

So knowing what's best in life doesn't entitle you to force others into what's best. Still, your friend's right to prefer banking doesn't stop its being true that music is better (if it is) or make it wrong for you to take account of that fact when deciding how much to support her after she's chosen. Thus, you may legitimately do more to encourage her career if it's in music rather than finance: you can prefer to help her with what's better. Nor is it in any way wrong for you to consider the respective merits of music, banking, or whatever when you're choosing a career for yourself. So long as you don't harm other people, their rights don't bear on your choice and you can assess your options mostly as they'd affect you. This self-regarding context isn't the only one in which questions of value arise, but it's both natural and common, and will often be the one we consider in this book.

Is pleasure good, and if so, is it the main ingredient in a good life or just a minor one? Is knowledge good in itself? What about love, or caring for someone who cares for you? Does being morally good make your life better? These questions are our subject—let's get to them.

Chapter One

FEELING GOOD

I feel good . . . I knew that I would now.

—James Brown

The most commonly recognized intrinsic good has several names: pleasure, happiness, enjoyment, contentment, satisfaction. But they all refer to a good feeling, a sensation with a positive tone that we like and usually want to get more of. And it has an opposite or bad feeling, called variously pain, suffering, and misery, with a tone we dislike and want to avoid. The theme of this chapter is that feeling good is good and feeling bad is bad. If you have innocent pleasures or enjoyments, that makes your life better; if you suffer pain, that makes it worse. Can anyone deny that?

I'll use the term "pleasure" for the whole class of good feelings and "pain" for all the bad ones. But whatever it's called, pleasure can't be defined in other terms. It's just any feeling with a felt quality of pleasantness: if you haven't experienced it, it can't be explained to you any more than the color blue can be explained to someone who's never seen blue. Do you want to know what pleasure is? Eat a chocolate, tan on the beach, or watch your favorite sports team win a championship, then look inside at what you're feeling. See that positive buzz? That's pleasure.

Though it's a feeling, pleasure isn't one you can experience on its own. If you eat a chocolate, you have a sensation of pleasantness, but it's mixed with other sensations of chocolate taste and creamy mouthfeel; if you tan, it goes with feelings of warmth on your back and relaxation in your muscles. And you can't separate out the pleasantness or concentrate on it by itself. (Try it if you don't believe me.) In each case the pleasantness is part of an indissoluble whole. So while you can experience chocolate pleasure and tanning pleasure and championship pleasure, you can't experience just pleasure, or pleasure by itself. Nothing is ever "pure pleasure," despite what people say.

Some philosophers have concluded from this that pleasure isn't a single feeling at all, or not one we can measure or try to get more of. But this doesn't follow. Compare the loudness of sounds. That's just as much something you can't experience on its own: you can't hear just loudness without the additional acoustic qualities of, say, a trumpet or a bass guitar. But loudness is still a quality of sounds and one we can rank them in. We can say the trumpet is louder than the bass guitar, which is louder than the piano. Similarly, we can say watching the championship was more enjoyable than the tanning, which was more pleasant than eating the chocolate. What you can't isolate can still be something you compare from feeling to feeling and try to get as much of as possible.

Though all pleasures share a felt quality of pleasantness, there are different types of pleasure. In this chapter I'll distinguish them from each other, ask whether any are better as pleasures, and explore how they interact with each other. But first there's another issue, about how pleasure relates to our desires.

DO WE WANT ONLY PLEASURE?

What's hard to deny is that pleasure is *one* intrinsic good and pain *one* evil. But some philosophers believe, more radically, that pleasure is the only good and pain the only evil, so what determines the quality of your life is only how good it feels. This view is called ethical hedonism, and it's often based on the psychological claim that what we want is ultimately only pleasure, or the greatest possible surplus of pleasure over pain for ourselves. This is psychological hedonism, and it concerns what we do want rather than what we ought to want. It would make a huge difference if it was true, so we need to decide if it is.

Psychological hedonism allows that we can want things other than pleasure but insists that when we do, we want them only as a means to pleasure. If we seek food or sex, it's only for the pleasure they'll give; if we want to play tennis or vacation in Prague, it's again only to get enjoyment. Even if we call 911 to help the victim of a car accident or we turn in a wallet we've found, it's only for the sake of a feeling: to get the pleasure of knowing we did something good or to avoid feeling guilty. In whatever we do, our ultimate aim is always our own pleasure.

If this were true, it would indeed follow, in a way, that pleasure is the only good. Ethics is supposed to help us decide how to live, or to steer us in better rather than worse directions. But this would be impossible if we were hardwired to aim only at our own pleasure. Then telling us that knowledge or moral virtue is good would be like telling water it should boil at some temperature other than 100 degrees centigrade; it could have no effect on what we do. Even the claim that pleasure is good would lose most of its interest. What would be the point of telling us we should aim at pleasure if we were always going to do that anyway? It would be like telling water *to* boil at 100 degrees.

Psychological hedonism looks scientific and appealingly unsentimental. It treats us as part of the natural world, biologically programmed, as many think other animals are, to seek only our own interest. It's also a debunking view. We may think we often act from noble motives such as altruistic concern for others' happiness or respect for moral principle, but that, hedonism says, is just pretense. Underneath, these acts all have the same selfish motive as eating and having sex: the desire for our own pleasure. So to accept psychological hedonism is to see through fantasies others are fooled by. (I think that's why I believed it as a self-important seventeen-year-old: it seemed so worldly-wise.)

But it's psychological hedonism that's the fantasy. Though pleasure is clearly one thing we want, the idea that it's the only thing we want squares with neither our felt experience nor current biological science.

Imagine that you see a car accident and call 911. As you dial, do you think, "I want pleasure, and it will give me pleasure to help this person, so I'll help"? Surely you do no such complicated thing; you just find yourself wanting to help. Or you're watching your favorite team play for a championship. Do you say, "I want pleasure, and it will give me pleasure if they win, so I hope they win"? Again not—you just want them to win. Psychological hedonism overcomplicates our mental life by making it involve reasoning that doesn't seem to be there; it makes us want things as means to an end when our experience is that we simply want them. A hedonist may say the desire for pleasure is still present and guiding us; it's just not conscious. But what's the reason to posit this unconscious desire? It can't be just because this is necessary to make psychological hedonism true; we're trying to decide *whether* it's true. And our experience is against it: we don't always find ourselves aiming at pleasure.

Moreover, we often do what we know will cost us pleasure. You can stop to help an accident victim even though you know it means missing a terrific concert, one that would give you more pleasure than you'll get from helping. You just think helping is more important. Nor does this happen only with altruistic desires. You can want an extra whiskey tonight even though you know it will cause you more pain tomorrow— you just want that whiskey now. Or consider a desire for revenge. Someone has mocked you and you want to pay him back—maybe hit him or say something really wounding. As you do so, you can know you'll pay for your action in the future and long regret what you've done. Even so, what you want most right now is to hit or wound him.

As the eighteenth-century philosopher Joseph Butler argued, psychological hedonism often gets things exactly backward. It's true that if you get what you want—if the accident victim is helped or your team wins—you usually feel pleased. But that's because pleasure usually follows from having your desires fulfilled, as an aftereffect. You don't first want pleasure, then believe that helping will give you pleasure, and then help. You first want to help, then do so, and afterward are happy that you did. Or you first want your team to win and then get pleasure when they do. I became a Montreal Canadiens fan when, in 1956, my father told me the best hockey player in the world had just had a career-threatening injury. The player was Maurice Richard, he was the Canadiens' star, and since then I've thrilled in their victories and suffered through their losses. I didn't decide as a four-year-old that I'd get pleasure if I wanted the Canadiens to win and on that basis develop that desire; I was caused to have it by my father's remark and later got pleasure when what I independently wanted came about.

As Butler said, we have desires for things outside us just as things outside us, and we often wouldn't get the pleasures we do without having those desires. How could you get pleasure from helping an accident victim unless you first wanted to help, or feel guilty about not helping unless you first cared about doing what's right? In the revenge case, how could it please you to hit or wound someone unless you independently wanted revenge against him?

Contemporary biology supports the same conclusion. Consider first animal behavior—say, that of a mother duck who distracts a predator away from her ducklings and toward herself. She's not promoting her own interest by doing this; she's putting her life at risk. But behaviors like hers are positively favored by natural selection. If she has a gene for acts of distracting predators, then at least half her offspring can be expected to share this gene. So if she sacrifices her life to save six ducklings, at least three copies of the gene will survive rather than one. And a gene that survives three times rather than one will more successfully replicate itself. At the level of genes, where selection happens, it can favor genes for altruism in animals.

Natural selection also favors simpler mechanisms for producing these behaviors. A mother duck could be hardwired to want only her own pleasure and to believe that distracting predators will give her pleasure, or hardwired directly to distract predators. The second mechanism will be faster, because it has fewer component parts, and for the same reason it's less likely to misfire. So selection should prefer it. And it's surely what we find: when a duck distracts a predator from her young, she does so just by instinct.

The same holds for humans. Imagine that it's adaptive for us to sometimes seek revenge, as many think it is. We could be hardwired to want only pleasure and to believe, when angry, that revenge will give us pleasure, or hardwired just to want revenge when angry. The second will again be the faster mechanism and less likely to misfire. So it's again what we should expect, and I've argued that it's what we find: when we're angry, we just want to hit or wound.

This even holds for the hedonists' favored desires, for food and sex. If you haven't eaten in three days, do you want to eat only as a means to pleasure or do you also want, more simply and ravenously, just to eat? Surely the latter. Wanting to eat as a means to pleasure is most common when you're feeling comfortable and, say, planning a gourmet meal. But biology also gives us, more elementally and more usefully in dire circumstances, a simple desire to eat.

Pleasure is certainly one thing we want, and getting pleasure when another desire is fulfilled reinforces that desire.

Even if we have an elemental desire for food, it's strengthened when eating turns out to be pleasant, as it obviously does. What's not true is that we want only pleasure as an end. We can want many things as ends, both inside our minds and out, and that leaves room for ethics to steer us toward some ends rather than others.

But why should it steer us toward pleasure, even if only as one good among many? Why should feelings with that particular quality be good? Here we come to the end of what philosophy can do. If pleasure is good, there won't be a further or deeper explanation why; it will just be true that a feeling's being pleasant makes it worth having. And to confirm that pleasure is good, we can only think about how it feels and ask whether, given that, it doesn't make your life better. But surely it does; surely contentment, happiness, and ecstasy are benefits. Or we can think about how pain feels and ask whether suffering, misery, and agony don't make a life worse. That's if anything more compelling.

Writing to a friend's newborn daughter, the poet Philip Larkin wished not that she be talented or beautiful but that she be ordinary: "In fact, may you be dull / If that is what a skilled, / Vigilant, flexible, / Unemphasised, enthralled / Catching of happiness is called." I'll assume that Larkin wasn't utterly misguided and that what he was wishing the young girl was indeed one of the best things in life.

PLEASURE: LET ME COUNT THE WAYS

Many things can make us feel good, and these can be different for different people. One person can get pleasure from chocolate ice cream while another prefers strawberry; one can enjoy wilderness canoeing while another likes knitting and a third is happiest at loud concerts. But alongside these differences in the sources of pleasure are differences among pleasures themselves. There are different types of good feeling—four, to be precise, generated by two cross-cutting divisions among pleasant sensations.

The first division is between pleasures that aren't "about" something and ones that are. The simplest pleasures, including all the bodily pleasures, aren't directed at anything beyond themselves; they're just feelings. When you experience one of these pleasures, you're not pleased *that* something is the case; you're just pleased, or have a self-contained pleasant sensation. This sensation may have various aspects, such as the additional felt qualities that make the pleasure of eating chocolate different from that of tanning. And in some cases there can be many such qualities, as when you eat a complex dish that balances many different flavors. But even then the pleasure doesn't point beyond itself to something external. It's just a feeling, however multifaceted, with no reference beyond the internal qualities you feel.

But other pleasures do point beyond themselves, because they *are* about something. You're not just pleased, you're pleased *that* something is the case: that the Canadiens won the championship, that your friend got a promotion, that the audience laughed at your jokes. You have a thought about some state of the world and take pleasure *in* that state, or *that* it holds. These "pleasures-that," as I'll call them, are more intellectually sophisticated than simple pleasures, because they require the capacity for complex mental representations. An animal can't be pleased that the Canadiens won, because it can't have thoughts about the Canadiens; maybe animals can't have any pleasures-that, only physical ones. But pleasures-that are still pleasures, because they still feel pleasant or involve a buzz. When you're pleased that the Canadiens won, you don't just think that they did; you do so *and* feel good about that fact. Your pleasure may not be very distinctive qualitatively or have as many internal aspects as that of eating a complex dish. What distinguishes pleasures-that from each other may be not how they feel but what they're about, such as a Canadiens win or a friend's promotion. But they still involve the shared quality of pleasantness, and their intensity can still be compared with that of other pleasures. You can say you were more pleased by your friend's promotion than by the Canadiens' win, or got more pleasure from it than from eating chocolate. A buzz about some fact is different from a simple buzz, but it's still a buzz.

The objects of pleasures-that are often things outside your mind, like a team's victory, but they can also be internal, as when you're pleased that you know calculus or glad that you love your spouse. They can therefore also include your own simple pleasures and pains. You can get physical pleasure from eating a chocolate and then feel a further pleasure *that* you're getting the physical one. The pleasure-that is a second pleasure, made possible by the first, and lets you double your pleasure. You can even feel pleasure-that in a simple pain, and that's what some masochists do. They first feel physical pain, say, from being spanked. Then, perhaps because they want the pain, they feel pleasure *that* they're feeling it, or feel good *that* they're feeling bad. And if the second pleasure is sufficiently intense, they can end up feeling more pleasure than they do pain, so they feel good on balance. This kind of masochism may be unusual, but it's certainly possible, and what makes it possible is the difference between simple feelings and ones directed at an object: you can feel pleasure that you're simply pained and thus get pleasure from your pain. (The converse case of pain at your own pleasure is even more unusual and may be possible only for someone who's deeply self-hating. But, again, it's possible.)

This first division among feelings is a sharp one: either a pleasure is about something or it's not. The second division is more one of degree and concerns how broad or extended your pleasure is. Consider a mild physical pleasure or pain. It's localized in some part of your body: you feel pleasure in your back when it's being massaged or a pain in your elbow if you bang it. And it occupies just one part of your consciousness. You can simultaneously feel the pleasure of the massage and the pain in your elbow while also having other thoughts and feelings, so each is just one element in your overall state of mind. If you think of your consciousness as a canvas, physical pleasures and pains are individual splotches of color at particular points on that canvas.

But other pleasures and pains pervade your consciousness. Think of a good mood, such as elation or, more mildly, contentment. It isn't localized; there's no specific part of the body where you feel elated or content. Nor is it just one item alongside others in your consciousness; it extends throughout your consciousness, coloring the whole as a blue wash can color the whole of a canvas. It lies behind your other mental states, giving your whole mind a positive tone. In the same way, sadness or depression gives your whole mind a negative cast, so you're gloomy not in any part of your body or about one thing but generally.

These moods are like physical pleasures in not being about anything; a contented or depressed mood can be caused by thoughts of something in the world, but in itself it's an object-less feeling. You're not contented about something; you're just contented. But moods differ from physical pleasures in pervading your consciousness, and the good ones are some-times given the special label "happiness." We wouldn't nor-mally say that someone who's now eating a chocolate is on that basis happy; though he's feeling a pleasure, he needs more to count as happy. But we might well call him happy if he's in an overall good mood, with a pleasant feeling filling his mind. The extra needed for happiness may well be a general-ized feeling rather than a localized simple one.

There's a related distinction for pleasures-that. Some of these have very particular objects: that a specific friend got a promotion today, that this audience laughed at that joke. But others are about something much more extended. You can feel pleased by everything that's going on around you or by the entire state of the world today—everything everywhere is great! But an important case is when you're pleased by your whole life, taking all its aspects together and considering your past, present, and likely future. Then you have what's called overall life satisfaction, or a good feeling about the total package of what you've done and experienced and will continue to. You needn't be pleased by every item in the package; looking back, you can feel regret and even shame about some things. But taking everything together and weighing the good against the bad, you feel positive about your life's course as a whole.

This more extended pleasure-that can also be called "happi-ness." We wouldn't normally say that someone who's pleased about a friend's promotion is on that basis in a state of happiness. (He may be happy about the promotion, but he's not simply happy—more is needed for that.) But if he has a good feeling about his whole life, in all its aspects and through time, that does seem like happiness. In fact, some philosophers have defined happiness as "satisfaction with one's existence as a whole." As with a mood like contentment, a good feeling that extends further, though now in its object rather than in how much of your mind it fills, better merits the name "happiness."

So there are four types of good feeling: simple pleasures that are discrete items in your consciousness, like the bodily pleasures of food and sex; simple pleasures that pervade your consciousness, like a good mood; pleasures-that with a particular object, such as a Canadiens win or a friend's promotion; and pleasures-that with a more extended object, such as your whole life. Since they all involve a positive tone, they're all pleasures and all desirable. But do they differ in value? Are some more worth seeking than others?

BETTER PLEASURES?

A simple view says no: the types of pleasure are all equally good. Each involves a positive buzz, and if their intensities of buzz are equal, so are their values. But some people may prefer certain types to others.

For example, some may say pleasures-that are better than simple pleasures because they're more intellectually demanding. Aristotle thought the good life for humans has to involve properties that are distinctive of us rather than shared by other animals; this was his main ground for valuing rationality as the supreme human quality. Pleasures-that satisfy this condition, since only we have the intellectual capacities to experience them. They are therefore properly human pleasures, some may argue, as against the merely animal pleasures of food and sex, and on that basis better.

But I'm not persuaded. First, there are problems about valuing properties because they're distinctive of our species. Right now we think only humans can reason, but what if we discover that dolphins can reason? Will that make reasoning no longer good in us? Or what if we encounter aliens who can reason? Surely the human good should depend only on facts about us and not on facts about other species.

More important, the distinctiveness argument doesn't value pleasures-that *as* pleasures. I agree that exercising our intellectual capacities is good, especially when it leads to knowledge; I'll discuss this in Chapter Four. But though the use of intellect is involved in pleasures-that, it's also separable from them and therefore a different value. Let's say I'm pleased that the Canadiens won. This involves a thought about the Canadiens that animals can't have, but I can think the same thought without any pleasure. I can think about their win but not have any feeling about it; I can just be neutral. Or I can be pained by the thought, as I may be if I hate the Canadiens. Any intellectual value in having the thought is the same in all three cases, but we're interested in what makes being pleased that the Canadiens won better than being neutral or pained by it. We're interested in the pleasure-that's value *as a pleasure*, and it's irrelevant to this if other, intellectual values go with it.

There's another irrelevant value a pleasure-that can have. Let's say you're pleased at something good—your friend is happy and you're pleased that he's happy. This is good in part because it's a morally fitting attitude toward something of value; it's a positive response to something good, which I'll argue in Chapter Six is virtuous and therefore also a good. But this good too is separable from the pleasure-that. Instead of feeling pleased that your friend is happy, you can want him to be happy when he's not. That also is virtuous because it's a positive attitude toward something good, and it's likewise virtuous to be pained by a friend's pain. So a pleasure-that in his happiness, while to some degree good as a pleasure, can also be good as virtuous. But we're only interested in the first kind of goodness, the one not shared by virtuous wants and pains.

To isolate this goodness, consider a pleasure in something neutral, like a Canadiens victory. (Though a fan, I'm not foolish enough to think their winning is intrinsically better than another team's winning.) And ignore any minor intellectual good involved in thinking of the victory. Is this pleasure-that, considered just as a pleasure, any better than an equally intense physical pleasure of eating chocolate or an equally intense good mood? I see no reason to believe this. Pleasures-that can involve other values, either intellectual or moral, but considered just for their value as pleasures, they don't seem any better. Given a simple pleasure and a pleasure-that of equal intensity, their value as pleasures seems the same.

Others may say the more extended pleasures are better. Thus, they may say a somewhat less intense overall good mood can be better than a more intense physical pleasure, because it fills more of your mind. Bentham identified two dimensions of value in a pleasure, its duration and its intensity, so a longer-lasting pleasure is better (sounds right), as is a more intense one (also right). The idea here is that there's a third dimension of value, breadth or extent, so a pleasure that fills all your consciousness is better than an equally intense one that's psychically localized.

Something like this idea may be implicit in our everyday talk of "happiness." This word has more positive connotations than "pleasure." "I seek happiness" sounds more reputable than "I want pleasure," and it's no accident that the Declaration of Independence speaks of "life, liberty, and the pursuit of happiness," not the "pursuit of pleasure"—that would seem tawdry. But if "happiness" sounds higher-class and we apply it more readily to feelings that pervade consciousness, that may suggest that we think these feelings are more desirable than localized simple pleasures.

A similar view is possible for pleasures-that, so a somewhat less intense feeling of satisfaction with your life as a whole can be better than a more intense pleasure in a particular fact. Again the former's greater extent, though now in its object rather than in how much of your mind it fills, is taken to give it more value. This view too may be implicit in our talk of "happiness." If we apply this word more readily to life satisfaction, that may again suggest that we think this type of pleasure is more valuable. Feeling pleased with your whole existence, we may be saying, is better than being equally pleased by something more specific.

I'm not sure what to think of these two views. (Questions about what's good are difficult, and this book won't answer them all.) If we think of a happy life, we do often think of it as involving lasting feelings of overall satisfaction rather than a succession of separate enjoyments. (One writer said, "Don't mistake pleasures for happiness. They're a different breed of dog.") But we need to be careful about why we think this.

Our overall mood and attitude toward our life can vary, going up and down as external events affect them. But they do this much less than physical pleasures and particular pleasures-that, which come and go more rapidly. If someone's in a good mood or feeling life satisfaction today, there's a better chance he'll be feeling the same way next week or next year than if he's now just eating a chocolate. And we may be influenced by this fact when we evaluate the types of pleasure, counting the more extended ones for more because we think they tend to last longer and are therefore better indicators of good feeling in the future. But we shouldn't do this. To compare the types of pleasures as types, we should consider them just as they're felt at a particular time, with no reference to the future. When we do that, do we really find more value in pleasures that fill consciousness or concern one's whole life than in equally intense particular ones?

I have to say I don't find this myself, and I therefore don't see any reason to abandon the simple view that the different types of pleasure are all equally good. Though pleasures can be divided into categories, what determines their value, duration aside, is always just their degree of pleasantness. This means that to determine how much total pleasure a person feels at a given time, we need to identify all his different good feelings at that time, measure (so far as we can) their intensities, and then, weighing the types of pleasure equally, add those measures together. (We can never do this in practice, but it's the ideal our rough measures approximate to.) The resulting sum gives his total pleasure at that time.

Given this procedure, two people can end up experiencing the same total amount of good feeling in very different ways. Consider on one side a fine-dining Lothario. He enjoys a succession of intense physical pleasures, both gustatory and erotic, but has doubts about how he's living—isn't it a bit ignoble?—and so feels little life satisfaction or general contentment. Now consider an ascetic monk. Though he has few physical pleasures, since he's not allowed them, his mood is always gently positive and he does feel life satisfaction. The Lothario enjoys mostly short-lived intense pleasures of one type, the monk milder enduring pleasures of a different type. Despite that, the total pleasure they enjoy may be roughly the same, so their lives feel on balance roughly equally good.

THE HAPPY GET HAPPIER AND THE SAD GET SADDER

Though the four types of pleasure differ, there are also connections between them. Sometimes one blends into another, and they regularly reinforce each other, so having one type of pleasure encourages you to have others. Being happy in one way tends to make you happy in others, just as, on the other side, sadness breeds more sadness.

Consider first a localized physical pleasure or pain. If it's mild, it's just one feeling among others, but as it gets more intense it can flood your consciousness, spreading through it and overwhelming all other sensations. (Think of a paint splotch spreading to fill a canvas.) This can happen with orgasm, on one side, and the pain of being tortured, on the other. The feeling is still based in part of your body, unlike a mood, but like a mood, it fills your mind.

Alternatively, a physical pleasure like that of a good meal can leave you with an overall feeling of contentment: stretching out luxuriantly, you not only feel good about the meal but also simply feel good. Here a localized pleasure causes a more extended one of mood. Conversely, an overall good mood makes you more receptive to physical pleasures, so you feel them more intensely; you enjoy your meal more when you're feeling up. Certainly the contrary mood of depression sucks the pleasure from food and even sex, and that's one of the worst things about depression: even physical thrills no longer please.

A good mood likewise promotes particular pleasures-that. Think of the common scene in movies where a character who's just fallen in love finds everything around him wonderful: a fire hydrant, the cop on the corner, the dog who usually bites him. Feeling generally elated, he sees more around him as worth delighting in. And a good mood makes you optimistic, so you tend to see the good side of things, while a bad mood does the opposite. Given a half-full mug, one person will see the beer it contains and will look forward to enjoying it, while another focuses on what's gone and can no longer be had. The one's optimism gives him a particular pleasure-that while the other's pessimism breeds regrets, and the difference between them may ultimately be one of mood, as the one who's up sees pluses and the one who's down sees minuses. (I myself am in the middle: I tend to see the glass as both half full and half empty, or to see something good in anything bad and something bad in anything good. This tendency is both good and bad for me.)

A similar point applies to memory. We remember best what we were attending to most at the time; if you ask Jack Nicklaus what iron he hit into the seventeenth green in the 1968 British Open, I bet he'll remember—he was concentrating that hard.

But this means that if optimists focus on good things and pessimists on bad, the former will have happy memories while the latter will have sad ones. An optimist will remember most the early, thrilling part of a love affair, a pessimist its bitter end; one will recall the sunny days on a vacation, the other the rain. It's sometimes said the key to happiness is a bad memory, but that's true only for pessimists; for optimists, good recall provides recurring joys.

A good mood can also make you feel satisfied with your life. The movie character who's just fallen in love thinks his whole life is fantastic, and the same often happens in real life. Asked to rate their life satisfaction on a scale from 1 to 10, people give a higher number if they're asked on a sunny day or right after finding a dime in the change tray of a photocopy machine. A particular event has made them feel overall good, which in turn makes them view their life more positively. Conversely, life satisfaction encourages a good mood: when you find your whole existence desirable, you generally feel content. And particular pleasures-that can do the same, as when feeling elated that the Canadiens won makes you feel simply elated.

In all these cases one type of pleasure directly promotes another. But there can also be indirect effects, when feeling good in one way leads you to do things you wouldn't do if you were gloomy, and these things then give you further pleasure. For example, optimists are more willing to try new experiences, such as new foods or a new sport like skydiving, which then give them new enjoyments. They're also more likely to approach people socially, so they end up with more friends, go to more parties, and perhaps have more sexual partners. Those who are less cheerful might enjoy these things just as much, but their being less cheerful makes them less likely to seek and find them.

Of the four types of pleasure, the most potent at promoting the others may be a good mood. Though affected a little by them, it plays a large role in opening us up for physical pleasures, prompting particular pleasures-that, and making us satisfied with our lives. This may be one reason why it's thought to be so important and is often referred to as "happiness"—it's a prime source of general good feeling.

But the main point is that, in various ways, the different types of pleasure reinforce each other, so someone who enjoys one is more likely to enjoy others. The happy tend to get happier and, sad to say, the sad get sadder. If you have one type of good feeling, you're likely to have others; lack one and you probably lack others.

But then how do you start on happiness? How do you break into the circle of good feelings? That's our next topic: how to get that wonderful buzz.

FURTHER READINGS

The idea that pleasure involves an indefinable felt quality of pleasantness is found in Jeremy Bentham's *Introduction to the Principles of Morals and Legislation*; that work also defends psychological hedonism and argues, on its basis, that pleasure is the only good. The classic critique of psychological hedonism is in Joseph Butler's *Fifteen Sermons*, while a more recent treatment is Joel Feinberg's "Psychological Egoism"; the biological case against hedonism is made in Elliott Sober and David Sloan Wilson, *Unto Others*. An account of good feeling that emphasizes an overall good mood, calling that "happiness" and making it the primary hedonic value, is in Daniel M. Haybron's *The Pursuit of Unhappiness*. Accounts that do the same for life satisfaction are in Hastings Rashdall, *The Theory of Good and Evil*, vol. 2, chap. 2; Robert Nozick, *The Examined Life*, chap. 10; and L. W. Sumner, *Welfare, Happiness, and Ethics*, chap. 6. The view that all four types of pleasure are equally good is closer to Bentham, who thought the only qualities relevant to a pleasure's intrinsic value are its duration and its intensity.

Chapter Two

FINDING THAT FEELING

I can't get no satisfaction.

—The Rolling Stones

If the types of pleasure reinforce each other, then if you have some, you're likely to get others. But how do you start to get those good feelings?

Some people think it's easy, because they think your feelings are under your voluntary control. A remark sometimes attributed to Abraham Lincoln says, "Most folks are about as happy as they make up their minds to be," suggesting that we need only to choose to be happy and we will be. Many self-help books assume the same: if you want good feelings, they'll be yours.

But I don't think many people who struggle with sadness or depression will agree. They don't find they can cheer themselves up just by wanting to, and in fact improving your level of happiness is usually very difficult. In part you've got, perhaps from birth, a set level of overall feeling that it's hard to move away from. In part many things that you think will give you pleasure don't have lasting effects. And many activities that do bring pleasure aren't ones where you seek pleasure directly. The wiser thought is Robertson Davies's "Happiness is always a by-product." Good feelings don't often come in the front door because you asked them to enter; they prefer to slip in the back door when and because you're absorbed in something else. The best route to good feeling is often indirect.

PLEASING YOURSELF

The most obvious way to feel good is to give yourself physical pleasures: eat chocolate, tan on a beach, do exercises that make your body hum, have sex. And these pleasures can add nicely to your life—think of the fine-dining Lothario. But there are limits to what they can do.

Of the types of pleasure, the physical ones do least to promote other pleasures: eating chocolate doesn't usually make you feel good about your life as a whole or prompt particular pleasures-that. And they tend to be short-lived. The pleasure of eating chocolate lasts only as long as the chocolate does, and even apart from that it tends to pall. If you eat your way through a stack of Mars bars, you'll get less pleasure from the second than from the first and by the sixth will probably be getting no pleasure at all.

Some philosophers have thought the physical pleasures aren't really pleasures at all—they're illusory. Plato, for example, thought they always start from a felt lack. Your body is short of water, so you feel thirsty, which is unpleasant; it lacks food, so you're hungry. When you drink or eat, you replenish the lack and remove the unpleasantness, but you mistake this process for a positive sensation. You think you're feeling positive pleasure when you're really just moving from the discomfort of a felt lack to the neutral feeling of being full. And this makes the pursuit of physical pleasure self-defeating. It requires the pain of hunger or thirst to get started and offers no real sensation in return.

This view is exaggerated. There's a positive felt quality to the pleasures of food and sex; orgasm isn't just like ceasing to feel pain. But there's a point behind Plato's exaggeration, since as well as being short-lived, physical pleasures often alternate with physical pains. Some pains come before the pleasure, like an addict's craving for another fix or the parched throat that precedes a cool drink. Others come after, like the hangover after a binge or the bloated feeling following a too-rich meal. And many physical pleasures do long-term harm to your health, so they cause even later pains.

Again, this point shouldn't be exaggerated. Sometimes the night's fun is worth the morning's hangover, and there need be no bloat after a meal of French proportions rather than American size; the hum of exercise goes with long-term benefits to your health. Still, however nice they are, the physical pleasures can't usually by themselves give you a large total of good feeling through time; though the icing on the cake of happiness, they're usually not the main layer.

Much more promising here is a good mood. As we've seen, it does a lot to promote other pleasures—for example, by making you optimistic—and it can last a long time. Since it also feels good in itself, improving your mood could significantly increase your total of good feeling. But can you do it?

Unfortunately, it's much harder than giving yourself a physical pleasure. Most of us find that our mood goes up and down in response to events in our lives, but the variations are usually short-lived, and we return fairly quickly to an everyday or set level of contentment, representing our typical cast of mind. This set level can be different for different people: one person can be usually cheerful while another is more subdued, so they have different default temperaments. But most of us have some such temperament or some baseline mood that we return to after variations up or down.

One piece of evidence for this is how consistent we are in our reports of our happiness through time. The best predictor of how happy we'll feel in the future, far better than our age, income, or marital status, is how happy we've felt in the past. And a plausible explanation is that we have a baseline level of overall good feeling from which we only temporarily depart. We're consistent in how happy we say we are because we keep returning to the same default mood, and this default seems to have a genetic basis. Identical twins raised in separate families report very similar levels of happiness, much closer to each other's than is the case with fraternal twins raised together. Despite their different environments, their shared genes seem to give them a shared temperament, or shared disposition to a certain set level of mood.

If this is true, it echoes much older psychological ideas. Up to the nineteenth century, the main medical theories explained people's personalities by the balance within them of four bodily fluids or "humors": blood, phlegm, black bile, and yellow bile.

Someone with a predominance of blood would be sanguine or cheerful, someone with black bile would be melancholy, and so on. Though no one now accepts the details of this theory, psychologists are returning to the idea of partly innate temperaments that strongly influence our everyday level of feeling. The mechanism the psychologists postulate may now be the distribution of electrical activity within the brain—happy people show more activity in the left frontal lobe than in the right, and for sad people it is the opposite—or its level of the neurotransmitter serotonin. But there's the same basic idea of a partly fixed temperament.

The more your temperament is fixed, however, the harder it is to permanently increase your happiness by improving your mood. To a considerable extent, you're stuck with the default feeling you've got. Though you'd be happier if you could change it, mostly you can't.

Now consider particular pleasures-that, especially those that come from getting something you want. Isn't this a route to greater happiness: find out what you really desire and then get it? Again, it's harder than it seems.

There are extreme cases where satisfying a desire gives you no pleasure, the thing you wanted turning to ashes in your mouth. They're what Oscar Wilde had in mind when he said, "There are only two tragedies in life: one is not getting what one wants, and the other is getting it." For even when satisfying a desire does give you pleasure, the feeling is often short-lived.

Consider money. In opinion surveys Americans say they're unhappier about their income than about anything else and call lack of money their greatest obstacle to living a good life. So they work long hours to earn a little more. But once you're out of poverty, the contribution money can make to your happiness isn't very large.

Since the 1950s, Americans' inflation-adjusted incomes have more than doubled, yet their reported levels of life satisfaction are essentially unchanged; they have larger houses, fancier cars, and more gadgets, but say they're no more contented. A large increase in their income seems to have had little effect on their happiness. The same holds in comparisons between developed countries: the wealthier ones are again no happier. It's true that within countries richer people say they're happier than poorer ones, but when factors correlated with income, such as control over one's work, are separated out, the effect of income on happiness is small. Money makes a large difference to how you feel when it lifts you from poverty to moderate material comfort; then it spares you physical discomforts and anxiety about your future. But past that point, more money doesn't make you much happier.

Why? One reason is that your attitude toward your income depends less on its absolute level than on how it compares to other incomes, either other people's or your own at earlier times. In one experiment Harvard students were asked whether they'd rather earn $50,000 a year while other people earned $25,000 or $100,000 while others earned $200,000. A majority—56 percent—preferred the first option even though it involves a lower absolute income, and it's understandable why. It's gratifying to earn more than others in your local group, such as your neighbors or co-workers, and galling to earn less. But then raising everyone's income, as in the United States since the 1950s, will have little effect on people's happiness if their income levels relative to each other don't change.

You also care how your income now compares with what it was before. Taking your past earnings as a baseline, you're pleased when you've surpassed them, or earned more this year than last. But the resulting pleasure doesn't last, because your new income becomes a new baseline you again want to surpass. Many people say they need only a little more income to be happy, say, 20 percent more than they now earn, so they can buy just a few more things. (I know I've often felt this.) But when they get the extra 20 percent, that becomes their new normal; they again need just 20 percent more to be happy, and the cycle repeats itself. Increasing their absolute income again has little lasting effect on their happiness: what they want is always more than before, and any new income just becomes a new before.

There's a general psychic mechanism at work here, of adaptation to change. Because we focus so much on changes in our situation, we can get used to many things once they're permanent features of our lives. This trait is often good for us. People who suffer serious injuries, for example by becoming paraplegic, eventually return if not quite to their previous level of happiness then to one surprisingly close to it. Their injury becomes part of their baseline situation, with less effect on their day-to-day feelings than changes up and down from the baseline; here their adaptability limits their loss.

But the same adaptability limits our opportunities for lasting pleasure. People who win a lottery get an initial spike of happiness but within six months are back to their previous level—the win has no long-term effect. Forty years ago many people were excited to be able to listen to music in stereo or watch color TV, but who notices those things now? Something new gives new pleasure, but the novelty quickly fades.

So there's again a limit on how much you can increase your happiness. Seeking and getting things you want can give you short-term joy, but often you'll soon take your acquisition for granted and start craving something else. At worst you can end up on a "hedonic treadmill," constantly seeking new things for the pleasure you're convinced they'll bring but repeatedly finding yourself back where you began.

Again, this point shouldn't be exaggerated. Just as it's not true that the pains before or after a physical pleasure always outweigh it, so it's not true that forming and then satisfying wants always gives you no benefit. Though they may be short-lived, the resulting pleasures are certainly real, and if they follow each other quickly enough, they can add significantly to your life. Still, these pleasures often don't last long, and the wants that precede them are sometimes painful. Remember that in surveys Americans say they're positively unhappy about their current incomes, or feel positively bad about them; in their pursuit of money they are on a hedonic treadmill.

The last type of pleasure is life satisfaction, but like your overall mood, it's very hard to improve. On one side, your attitude toward your life depends on what your life has been like, and not only can you not change your past, but the changes in your future needed to increase your satisfaction ten years from now are very substantial. You'd have to do a lot of things differently to feel much better about yourself then. On the other side, your attitude toward your life also depends on your temperament. Two people can lead very similar lives, but if one's an optimist, he'll rejoice in the good things he's done, while a pessimist mostly regrets what she's missed. As we saw, however, your temperament isn't easy to change—that influence on life satisfaction is to a large degree fixed.

So feeling better is nothing like as easy as the self-help books say. The pleasures that would make a big difference to your level of feeling, such as an overall good mood or life satisfaction, are hard to get more of, while many that are easier to get give less of a lasting kick. But it doesn't follow that you can do nothing whatever to increase your happiness.

For one, you can avoid physical pains and things you don't want and never will adapt to, such as loud noise, having no control over your work, and a long commute in heavy traffic. No matter how many times you experience these, studies show, they never stop being nasty.

Another is to pursue things you want mostly for themselves, or aside from comparisons with other people and times. Asked whether they'd rather have two weeks' vacation while others have one week or four weeks while others have eight, a majority of the same Harvard students who preferred the lower income said they'd prefer the four weeks. Their attitude toward vacation time, unlike that toward money, wasn't based mainly on comparisons with other people. Similarly, if you had a choice between two nights a week with good friends while others have one night and three nights while they have four, surely you'd take the three nights. So giving everyone the same increase in their vacation or socializing time *would* increase their happiness; unlike a similar increase in income, it would do real good.

The same holds for choices we make as individuals. Vacations and social time are certainly things we want, just as we want money. So it's not inevitable that we spend as much time as we do on the last of these and so little on the first two—we could do things differently. In part we overestimate how much better some extra income will make us feel; in part there are pressures, from advertising and other media, that push us toward material consumption. But if we resist these pressures and think clearly about the future, we can pursue things that won't, once attained, yield so quickly to new dissatisfactions.

Finally, we can focus on a specific type of pleasure that's less prone to alternate with pains: enjoyment.

ENJOYING ACTIVITY

An enjoyment is a pleasure-that with a special kind of object, one indicated by the way we talk about it. When we're being most careful, we say we enjoy *doing* something, like playing golf or solving crossword puzzles. (Saying more simply that you enjoy golf is shorthand for the longer claim.) So the object of an enjoyment is always an activity, or something you do, and the activity has to be *yours*; you can't enjoy someone else's playing golf. (You can enjoy watching her golf, but then the watching is your activity.) So an enjoyment is a pleasure-that in a doing of yours. You're pleased to be engaged in this activity, and your pleasure can have as many aspects as the activity does. You can enjoy not only golfing but also hitting your drive on the tenth hole, walking down the fairway, and sinking your putt. Your pleasure in a complex activity can combine pleasures in the many subactivities it involves.

To fully enjoy an activity you have to be absorbed in it; if you're only half attending, you'll get only half the pleasure. You need to be immersed in your golf or crossword, to focus totally on it. Taken to the extreme, this results in what psychologist Mihaly Csikszentmihalyi calls "flow."

In a flow experience you're so absorbed in what you're doing that you have no awareness of anything around you. You also lose your sense of self. Your actions become almost automatic, with no thought of yourself as a separate agent performing them; you merge into the activity. But you also have a sense of power and control: you know that whatever the situation demands of you will get done. Your sense of time changes, either speeding up or slowing down, and you have an overall sense of calm, leading Csikszentmihalyi to call flow the most complete form of enjoyment.

Flow is possible in many activities: sports, music, chess, writing. And it sometimes comes to those of us with only modest skills. Playing hockey (which I did badly), I would sometimes get the puck in front of the other team's net and see it as just obvious what I had to do next—say, shoot into the bottom right corner, which the goalie was leaving open. Time would slow—though I had only a split second, I felt I could take whatever time I needed and was sure to do the right thing. And yes, I did score.

But flow comes most often to those with the highest skills. They have more to concentrate on: at any time they're exercising more abilities and doing so at a higher level, hitting more precise targets with their golf shots or making sweeter sounds on their violin. They more often feel control because they have more control; with greater talent come more occasions for absorption in an activity. Yet flow isn't something they adapt to or that fades over time, like the pleasure of another Mars bar. Their later rounds of golf or musical performances are sufficiently different, or remain sufficiently demanding, that the experience recurs.

At whatever level of skill, flow requires a balance of conditions. On one side, your activity has to involve some significant challenge; if it didn't, it wouldn't absorb your attention. But it can't be so difficult that the task is beyond you and you just feel frustrated. The root of flow is the successful exercise of a developed skill, which requires the right balance between challenge and ability.

It's actually debatable whether flow, while it's happening, involves the good feeling I've called pleasure. Csikszentmihalyi seems to think so, saying one aspect of flow is "a deep sense of enjoyment." And after the experience you often think, "That was exhilarating!" But if you're entirely focused on an outer activity, how can you at the same time be having an intense inner feeling of pleasure? Where's the psychic room for any great buzz? Some psychologists therefore deny that flow experiences are significantly pleasant while they're happening. When they're over, you feel excited about the non-hedonic aspects of what you did, such as the skill you exercised. You then transfer that excitement to the earlier time, assuming that if you're now thrilled by what you did, you must have felt thrilled then. But the transfer is a mistake, these psychologists say; at the time, you were too busy to be pleased.

There's another possibility: maybe while in the flow experience you do feel significant pleasure but are too absorbed to notice it fully. It's there but on the periphery of your consciousness, something you're partly aware of but don't take in in its entirety. Once the activity is over, you relax your concentration and realize how good you were feeling then. The activity really was deeply enjoyable; you just didn't know it at the time.

This analysis presupposes that you can have pleasures you aren't fully aware of, which may seem odd. But I don't see that it's impossible. (Can't the song "If you're happy and you know it, clap your hands!" state two separate conditions for clapping?) If it's not, you can be so absorbed in an activity that you're not fully aware of how good it's making you feel.

Even so, the pleasure in flow can't be that intense. If it were, you'd surely notice it more and it would disrupt your concentration. But at the same time flow pleasures are extremely pure. Just because you're so absorbed, you're not troubled by everyday worries and often don't notice physical pains, including those the activity itself causes. (Think how athletes playing a key game don't notice their bumps and bruises.) Even at moderate intensity, flow pleasure can give you a very good feeling.

And of course flow is just the extreme case of enjoyment, which has less radical forms. Even if your golfing or music doesn't take you completely out of yourself, it can involve considerable focus on an activity and, with that, considerable pleasure. Maybe it can even give you more pleasure than flow; maybe if you're not entirely concentrated on what you're doing, you're more able to feel the buzz it gives.

At whatever level, enjoyment isn't as hard to give yourself as other types of pleasure. While not unending, it's not as short-lived as physical pleasure, often lasting for hours rather than minutes. It's also less prone to the alternation with pain that Plato emphasized. What precedes enjoyment is often eager anticipation rather than a painful lack; what follows it is often not a down but a warm feeling of satisfaction with what you've done.

Enjoyments are also less based on comparisons than other pleasures-that and therefore are less likely to be undermined by them. Many people thoroughly enjoy golf despite knowing they're nowhere near as good as Tiger Woods or even the other players in their foursome; while playing they just forget that fact. Comparisons with your own past are more common. It's thrilling to be playing better than you've played before and frustrating to play worse. But again this effect seems less strong than with money—look at all the senior golfers and hockey old-timers, still getting a kick from a game they used to play much better.

Finally, it's easier to give yourself enjoyments than to improve your overall mood or attitude toward your life. If there's an activity you enjoy, just find time and do it. If you haven't found one yet, try some new pursuits—golf, crosswords, the violin—until one catches your fancy, and then throw yourself into it. Let it absorb you, and the good feeling will come. This brings us to a final truth about the pursuit of pleasure.

SEEK AND YE SHALL NOT FIND

Let's say you want to enjoy playing hockey, not necessarily at flow level but as much as you can. Will this happen if, while you play, you constantly monitor your level of pleasure and decide what to do next by asking what will most increase it? Crossing the blue line, you ask whether you'll get more pleasure from passing the puck to your winger or taking a slap shot, and then act on your answer. Is this how to get the most fun from hockey?

Surely not. Concentrating that much on your pleasure will detract from it by focusing your attention inward, rather than outward on the game and what it demands. To really enjoy hockey you have to care most about winning or just playing well and let your pleasure come as a side effect of doing that. You won't get the most enjoyment if you seek it directly; you have to aim at something else and let your pursuit of that give you the buzz.

This is odd. If pleasure is good, then you ought to pursue it, but if you do pursue it, you won't get as much of it as you could. Philosophers call it the "paradox of hedonism": that the best way to get pleasure is by not trying to. But the underlying point is more general. Pleasure can be one of what political scientist Jon Elster calls "states that are essentially by-products," ones you can achieve only as a side effect of seeking something else.

Consider respect. If you try consciously to win other people's respect and they see that you're doing so, they're less likely to respect you. Why should they esteem someone so feeble as to need esteem from them? To get their respect, you have to pursue some other worthwhile goal and let them admire you for how you do that. Or think of meaningful political activity. That again can't be achieved on its own—you can't just say, "Let's do something meaningful"—but only as a by-product of pursuing something else, like justice or equality, and letting that give your actions meaning.

Wherever it applies, the paradox of hedonism limits, if not the value of pleasure, then how much it should figure in your thinking. To get the most pleasure you shouldn't consciously seek it or even think of it as good; if pleasure is not to be out of sight, it must be out of mind.

We shouldn't exaggerate this point. The paradox of hedonism doesn't apply to all pleasures, and in particular not to physical ones like those of food and sex. Far from reducing your pleasure, it can heighten your thrill if you focus intently on the sensations provided by a complex dish or sexual stimulation. These pleasures absolutely can be sought directly. Nor does the paradox apply much to a good mood. While attending consciously to an overall up feeling may dampen it a little, it doesn't do so a lot.

The paradox does govern life satisfaction: to be pleased with your life, you have to first live a life you'll be pleased by. But its main application is to enjoyments or pleasures-that in your own activities. These pleasures require a focus away from your pleasure and onto the associated activities, because without the activities there's no good feeling, and they demand your attention. It's not that you can't be at all aware of your enjoyment; you can, to a limited degree. But your main focus has to be on what you're doing and not on how you feel.

This connects with our earlier critique of psychological hedonism. In Chapter One I argued that we don't want only pleasure as an end and other things just as means to pleasure; sometimes we want other things first and get pleasure only as a side effect of getting them. Now I'm saying this happens especially in enjoyments and even has to happen if we're to get the most pleasure they can give. To enjoy hockey the most, you have to first want to win or play well and let the good feeling come on the side; wanting hockey only as a means won't work. So we should actually be glad psychological hedonism isn't true, because if it were, we wouldn't get as much pleasure as we do.

There's another way the paradox shouldn't be exaggerated. What reduces your pleasure in hockey is thinking about it while you're playing; doing so at other times doesn't have that effect. So you can hope you'll enjoy a hockey game before you put on your skates and even decide to play because you think it will be fun, so long as you stop thinking about your enjoyment once you're on the ice. And most of us can do that. We can choose activities in advance for the pleasure they'll bring but lose ourselves in them once they start. We've somehow learned to turn off, at the right time, the concern with pleasure that would reduce the amount we get.

But even here the paradox plays a role. Our attitudes toward pleasure and pain are strongly time-biased—we care much more about pleasure in the present or near future than in the distant future. We'll choose a smaller pleasure now over a larger one far away—say, a chocolate bar now rather than two a year from today. So imagine that your hockey game is at eleven o'clock at night (as a lot of mine were) and it's now nine and you're watching TV. The show you're watching isn't great, but it's mildly enjoyable and the couch is comfortable. And to get to the game you have to get up, collect your equipment, and drive half an hour through dark, unattractive suburbs. If you care only about the pleasure the hockey will give you, will you do all that? Will you rouse yourself from your mildly pleasant idleness? Even if the game will be more fun than the TV, you may not, just because the hockey pleasure is more distant. But you'll be more likely to go play if you have other motives for doing so that are less time-biased, such as helping your team win, playing well, or not letting your teammates down. If even in advance you want more from hockey than pleasure, you're more likely to get the pleasure the game can give.

There's a further implication of the paradox. Enjoyment usually rests on the exercise of skill, which requires you to have enough skill to make your activity go smoothly. But that often means doing laborious rote exercises beforehand, such as skating drills or piano scales, that aren't particularly pleasant. Even apart from that, your first attempts at an activity are usually more frustrating than rewarding. If you're writing your first piece of fiction, you'll struggle to devise a plot, compose stylish sentences, and so on. And the frustration these efforts involve will probably outweigh the limited satisfaction you take in what you produce—since you're a beginner, it won't be very good—so you have more bad than good feelings through the process. But if you keep at your writing and improve, composing will become easier and your products will get better; over time, your satisfaction in what you write will come to outweigh any pains of producing it. And if you persist long enough, each piece of writing can make a large net contribution to your happiness, with just mild frustration leading to deep satisfaction. At the start it's a lot of pain for little pleasure; later on it's the opposite.

Given these facts and your time bias about pleasure, will you do the initial hard work of learning to write if you care only about the pleasure writing can give? Isn't that pleasure pretty far in the future? You're more likely to keep going through the initial frustrations if you have other supporting motives, such as a desire to write fiction for its own sake or to become known for your writing—particularly if those are your primary motivations and your interest in pleasure is only secondary.

This is especially so since physical and other passive pleasures often show the opposite pattern, going from most intense when they're first experienced to less so later on. The clearest illustration is addictive drugs. Your first experience of heroin is a fantastic high followed by only a minor letdown, so your net feeling through the process is massively positive. As you take more heroin, however, your tolerance for it increases and you get less of a high from the same amount; at the same time, your down when you come off it gets worse, so eventually the net feel of the experience, combining the high and the low, becomes negative. At the end you're taking heroin more to escape the horror of withdrawal than to get pleasure, so the habit's overall effect on your happiness is now strongly negative.

Something less extreme can happen with other consumption-based pleasures. Their sources may not become on balance painful, like heroin, but the pleasure they provide can pall, as you become jaded by repetition. Your hundredth time being driven in a fast sports car is nothing like as exciting as your first time; likewise with your hundredth time watching a TV game show. With these pleasures, the earliest are best and the later less good.

The contrast this makes with active enjoyments reinforces the paradox of hedonism. If you can either struggle to write your first fiction or try a new sports car, you have a choice between an option that's now at its least pleasurable and another that's now at its best. The first option will give you more pleasure over time if you stick with it, but if you want only pleasure and prefer it closer in time, you may well choose the second. It's only with other motives, such as a desire to write for the sake of writing, that you'll pick the first and get the most good feeling you can.

The paradox of hedonism doesn't apply to physical pleasures and can be avoided for enjoyments if you stop thinking about your pleasure when your activity starts. But our psychology often makes us less likely to get pleasure if we aim at it directly. We'll get more if we care mainly about something else, such as writing or playing hockey, and let the feeling come as a side effect. As Bette Davis is reported to have said, "A sure way to lose happiness . . . is to want it at the expense of everything else."

It follows that, to get the most pleasure, we should often have the desire for pleasure play a lesser role in our motivations. And this will be easier if pleasure has lesser value, so it's not the only or the most important good in life. If writing and hockey also have value, we have an additional reason to seek them: that they're good in themselves. In focusing on them, we're not turning away from what's good but may be seeking what's best. That pleasure does have this lesser value is our next topic.

FURTHER READINGS

Accessible recent surveys of the psychology of happiness that I have used in this chapter are Robert H. Frank, *Luxury Fever*; Daniel Gilbert, *Stumbling on Happiness*; Richard Layard, *Happiness: Lessons from a New Science*; Daniel Nettle, *Happiness: The Science Behind Your Smile*; and Martin E. P. Seligman, *Authentic Happiness*. Mihaly Csikszentmihalyi examines flow in *Flow:*

The Psychology of Optimal Experience. The paradox of hedonism is discussed in Henry Sidgwick, *The Methods of Ethics*, bk. 2, chap. 3, and Jon Elster discusses the more general phenomenon of "states that are essentially by-products" in *Sour Grapes: Studies in the Subversion of Rationality*, chap. 2.

Chapter Three

THE PLACE OF PLEASURE

The thrill is gone.

—B. B. King

Given the paradox of hedonism, we'll often get most pleasure if we aim mainly at something else, and that will be easiest if the something else is good. I'll soon argue that this is often the case: that many things other than pleasure have value. But first I'll note two ways that pleasure is a limited value even in its own domain. Even among feelings, it isn't most or even always that important.

PLEASURE VS. PAIN

First let's compare pleasure to its opposite, pain. I use "pain" to refer to all bad feelings, as I use "pleasure" for all good ones, and pains again come in four types. There are physical pains, localized in part of your body and discrete items in your consciousness; the more extended simple pain of a bad mood, such as depression or gloom; particular pains-that, such as that your friend lost her job; and life dissatisfaction, where you feel bad about your life as a whole.

Like pleasures, the types of pain can blend into each other and often reinforce one another. Persistent physical suffering can put you in a bad mood, as can a particular pain-that, while depression makes you more prone to physical pains and feelings of disappointment, both about particular things and about your whole life.

There are also, as with pleasures, questions about how the types of pain compare in value. Some may say the more extended pains, of a bad mood or of life dissatisfaction, are worse than the localized ones, but I see no reason to believe this. Given the same intensity and duration, the four types seem equally bad. This means there can be lives that, despite containing different kinds of pain, contain similar total amounts of it. One person may suffer many physical pains but not feel bad about his life as a whole, perhaps because he's proud of how he deals with his pain. Another can have few physical discomforts but be persistently unhappy about his life, perhaps because he thinks he's wasted his talents. Though the types of bad feeling they experience are different, their total bad feeling through time may be roughly the same.

But we also need to compare the values of the pains with those of pleasures. If you can enjoy an intense pleasure at the cost of a minor pain, it's surely worth doing so; if it's a mild pleasure at the cost of agony, that's a bad bargain. But how exactly do we make these comparisons, or weigh good against bad feelings?

Some philosophers have a simple view: since the painfulness of pains is the opposite of the pleasantness of pleasures, the two should be weighed equally against each other, so a pleasure of a given intensity is always exactly as good as a pain of the same intensity is evil. This was the view of Bentham and his fellow utilitarians, and it makes pleasure as great a good as pain is an evil. But I don't think this is right.

Imagine a world containing only intense mindless pleasures, such as those of eating chocolate. (I make them mindless so there won't be anything else such as knowledge that could give this world value.) If we ask whether this is a good world, one whose existence is better than if there were nothing, the answer is surely yes. But if we ask whether it's a very good world or only somewhat good, it seems to me that it's only somewhat good. Though it's better for there to be intense mindless pleasure than for there to be nothing, it's not fantastically better. A world with only this kind of pleasure isn't one to get very excited about.

Now imagine a world containing only intense mindless pain, say, that of being tortured. This is surely a very bad world, and vastly worse than nothing; it contains not just modest but massive intrinsic evil. But if that's so, the values of pleasure and pain *aren't* equal. Pleasure of a given intensity is less good than pain of the same intensity is bad, and pleasure is a lesser good than pain is an evil.

Or consider a more realistic case. Imagine that one person is suffering intense pain, so he's at −10 on a pleasure-pain scale (where larger negative numbers indicate greater degrees of pain), while another enjoys great pleasure and is at +9. And imagine that you can make the same small improvement in either's feelings, reducing the one's pain to -9 or increasing the other's pleasure to $+10$. If pleasure and pain had equal value, it wouldn't matter which you did; either choice would be as good. But surely that's not true; you should prefer reducing the first person's pain. If so, pain is again the more important value.

This view has been defended by several philosophers. G. E. Moore said that while pain is "a great evil," pleasure has at most "some slight intrinsic value"; Karl Popper wrote, "Human suffering makes a direct moral appeal, namely the appeal for help, while there is no similar call to increase the happiness of a man who is doing well anyway." Both recognized an asymmetry whereby the pain's negative value is greater than the pleasure's positive value, and in fact their view can be extended.

Imagine that you can either reduce one person's pain by one unit, from -10 to -9, or reduce another's by two units, from -3 to -1. If changes in pain always had the same value, it would be better to make the second reduction, because it's bigger. But that again doesn't seem right: it seems better to make the smaller reduction in the first person's pain, because his pain is worse. This suggests that not only is pain more evil than pleasure is good, but more intense pains are disproportionately more evil than less intense ones. Making a given change in a major pain makes a bigger difference than making the same change in a minor one.

There's a related view about pleasure. If you can improve one person's pleasure from $+1$ to $+2$ or another's from $+8$ to $+10$, it seems more important to do the former. Even though it's a smaller absolute increase in pleasure, it matters more because the first person starts with less. But then, whereas the evil of increases in pain gets greater as the pain gets more intense, the goodness of increases in pleasure gets smaller and may even diminish toward zero. If someone is already feeling total ecstasy, it may not matter more than infinitesimally that he feel even better.

These various views about pleasure and pain can be brought together in a diagram (Figure 3.1). Here the vertical axis measures value, with points higher up representing more value, while the horizontal axis measures pleasure and pain, with more intense pains further to the left of the origin and more intense pleasures further to the right. The curve shows how the value of a pleasure or pain varies with its intensity, and does so in a way that captures all the views we've been discussing. In the bottom left part of the diagram, the fact that the curve gets steeper as it goes down reflects the idea that a fixed increase in pain adds more evil the more intense the initial pain is, so the difference in value between −9 and −10 units of pain is greater than between −1 and −3. In the top right, the fact that the curve flattens means that a fixed

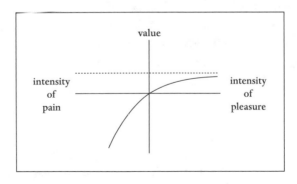

Figure 3.1

increase in pleasure gets less good the more pleasure you have; here the move from +1 to +2 adds more value than that from +8 to +10. Taken as a whole, the curve reflects the view that it's better to make the same fixed improvement in the feelings of someone who feels worse, because he feels more pain or less pleasure or feels pain rather than pleasure.

The curve therefore expresses a certain egalitarianism, telling us to care more about helping those who are worse off, and even to benefit them at the cost of those more fortunate. (If moving a badly off person from −10 to −9 will cause someone better off to drop from +10 to +8, we absolutely should do it.) But it also makes pleasure a lesser good than pain is an evil, since a pleasure of a given intensity is always less good than a pain of the same intensity is evil: the point for a mild pain is further below the horizontal axis than that for a mild pleasure is above it, as is the point for an intense pain compared with that for an intense pleasure. The diagram therefore captures Moore's and Popper's asymmetry, as well as our judgments about the two worlds with mindless feelings. The world with intense mindless pleasure is above the horizontal axis and therefore good, but it isn't and can't be very far above it, so it can't be very good. But the world with intense mindless pain is very far below the axis, and very evil.

Even in its own domain, then, pleasure is a limited value: though good, it's not as good as its opposite, pain, is evil. Even among feelings, it sits in second place.

THANK GOD THAT'S OVER

A second limit on the importance of pleasure concerns its location in time. Earlier I said we're time-biased because we care more about pleasures in the present or near future than in the distant future. But we also care less about pleasures and pains in our past. To see this, consider a striking example from the philosopher Derek Parfit.

You're in hospital for an operation that's extremely painful but can't be performed with anesthetics. Because of this, doctors induce short-term amnesia in patients afterward, so they won't know how much they suffered. You wake up in the hospital one morning with no memory of going to sleep and ask a nurse whether your operation is over or still to come. She says she's not sure: you're either a patient who had a very long, very painful operation yesterday or another patient who will have a much shorter operation today. You either suffered ten hours of agony yesterday or will suffer for one hour today. She goes off to see which you are.

If you weren't time-biased, you'd hope you were the second patient, who will have less suffering in his life as a whole. But surely none of us could do that—we'd hope fervently that we were the first patient, whose suffering is over. We'd rather have more pain in our life if only it was in our past; that kind of pain we can handle. And we have a similar attitude toward pleasure. Imagine learning that you either got a wonderfully pleasant surprise last year or will get a mildly pleasant surprise this year. Won't you want the second to be true, so your pleasure is still to come? You'll prefer less total good feeling in your life so long as you haven't yet had it.

These examples show that we care much less about pleasures and pains once they're behind us. (We say "Thank God that's over" when all that's happened is that a pain has moved from our present or future into our past.) Yet we don't think the same way about other things such as knowledge, achievement, and virtue.

Imagine that, in a variant of our example, you awake unsure of your identity and are told that you're either a scientist who made an immensely important discovery last year or another scientist who will make a minor discovery this year. Won't you hope you're the first scientist, who made the more important discovery last year? You'll want the greatest scientific achievement in your life, regardless of when it happens. Or imagine learning that you either committed a horrible moral wrong last year or will commit a lesser wrong this year. Won't you hope the second is true, because then your life will contain less wrongdoing? Past achievements still matter to us now, so we continue to feel proud of them after the fact; past failings also linger, causing us lasting guilt or shame. But past pleasures and pains do so much less; these feelings matter far more to us when they're here or ahead of us than when they're behind us.

Some philosophers have even said past pleasures have no importance. For Kant, "the pleasures of life do not fill time full, but leave it empty"; live for pleasure, and "the appearance of fullness will be confined to the present. Memory will find it empty." E. F. Carritt said a pleasure leaves us "never satisfied," whereas "an honest act, a scientific discovery, the creation of a beautiful thing, . . . are in a sense joys forever." Or as the workout T-shirt puts it, "Pain is temporary, pride is forever."

The same idea may figure in the common literary portrayal of a voluptuary at the end of his life: having lived mainly for pleasure, he screams in terror at the approach of death. The point of the portrayal is often religious: knowing he's sinned, the voluptuary dreads the hellfire to come. But it can also be non-religious. If your life has been one of virtue and achievement, then even though you now face an eternity of nothingness, it will always be true that you helped those people and accomplished those goals. Just as those facts remain important to you now, so they'll remain important in the future and forever be a counterweight to the oblivion ahead. But if you've lived only for pleasure, your past pleasures mean nothing now and there's no counterweight to the coming oblivion: just nothingness behind you like the nothingness ahead. And that can indeed make you scream.

One philosopher, T. H. Green, used this idea to argue that pleasure has no value at all. If something is truly good, he said, it must seem important to us at all times, not just times simultaneous with or before it but also ones that come after. If pleasure doesn't meet this condition—if it doesn't give "abiding satisfaction"—it isn't really good.

But Green, like Kant and Carritt, exaggerated the phenomenon. While we certainly care less about past pleasures and pains, I think we do care about them to some degree. If the nurse says that yesterday you had either a very long operation or a much shorter one, won't you hope you had the shorter one? If so, you must care at least some about past pains. And we can still get some pleasure from thinking of past enjoyments: time doesn't reduce their importance to nothing. (I still get a glow remembering a meal at a three-star restaurant in France in 1971.)

Moreover, we're not similarly biased about other people's past feelings. If you learn that your daughter either had a very painful operation yesterday or will have a less painful one today, won't you hope she'll have the less painful one today? If so, you care closer to equally about pains at all the times in her life; your bias mostly concerns just your own past feelings.

And this bias can be given a biological explanation. Alongside their intrinsic value, pleasure and pain have biological functions, the one reinforcing behaviors that promote our health and reproductive success while the other diverts us from behaviors that are harmful. But since these functions concern only the present and future—we can't do anything about our past health or reproduction—they'll fulfill it best if they direct our concern only to the present and future. Too much attention to the past would distract us from what we need now, and biology doesn't let us be distracted.

But then our discounting our past feelings needn't bear on their true value. Pleasure can indeed be ultimately good and pain evil; it's just that we're biologically programmed to care less about them in ourselves once they're behind us. It's not their merit that grounds our present indifference but their biological role.

Even so, there are grounds for doubt about pleasure's degree of value. Desiring something and believing it's good are different; we've all had the experience of intensely wanting something we know has little worth. But the two often go together, so wanting something tends to make us think it has value, or more value than we otherwise would. And it may be that while biology makes us care less about past pleasures and pains than their value merits, it also makes us care more about present ones than they merit.

If asked about the value of a pleasure or pain, we're most likely to imagine it as present—what would it be like to be having that feeling now? But the present is when pleasure and pain play their biological roles and when it's biologically most useful for us to care about them. In imagining them as present, may we not then exaggerate their value, so they're not really as good as we then take them to be? The same biological explanation that lets us discount our dismissal of past feelings may also diminish the significance of our concern for present ones. That we sometimes think pleasure and pain states are very important may be just as much an artifact of our evolutionary past as the fact that we're sometimes indifferent to them.

Whatever it means for the value of pleasure or pain, our bias against past feelings reinforces the paradox of hedonism. It implies that if we seek and get just pleasure, the benefit to us even in hedonic terms will be comparatively short-lived. We may get an immediate buzz, but since past pleasures matter little to us, we won't feel much gratification later. But if we aim at achievement or virtue, we may get a lesser initial kick but more lasting satisfaction: what feels less good at first may give more total pleasure through time. And the converse holds for pain. Even if seeking achievement or virtue hurts in the short term, the pain will be forgotten, while pleasure in the achievement persists—just as the T-shirt says.

So not only will aiming directly at pleasure now give you less pleasure now, but getting only pleasure now will give you less pleasure later, because pleasure isn't something there's much joy in recalling.

There are experimental illustrations of this. The psychologist Martin Seligman asked his students to do one pleasurable activity and one virtuous activity and then write about them both. He reports: "The afterglow of the 'pleasurable' activity (hanging out with friends, or watching a movie, or eating a hot fudge sundae) paled in comparison with the effects of the kind action. When our philanthropic acts were spontaneous and called upon personal strengths, the whole day went better. One junior told about her nephew phoning for help with his third-grade arithmetic. After an hour of tutoring him, she was astonished to discover that 'for the rest of the day, I could listen better, I was mellower, and people liked me much more than usual.'" She got more good feeling even in one day by first getting something else. That's because the pleasure of pleasure, unlike that of achievement or virtue, quickly fades.

BAD PLEASURES AND GOOD PAINS

Even if pleasure is less good than we sometimes think and less good than pain is evil, it could still be that the only real values are good and bad feeling. This is ethical hedonism, the view that only pleasure is good and only pain evil. It was held in the ancient world by Epicurus—hence our term "epicure" for a lover of food—and more recently by utilitarians such as Bentham and Henry Sidgwick. It remains the most popular view among those who say there's only one ultimate good.

Some have based ethical hedonism on psychological hedonism, the claim that all we ever want is our own pleasure, but we saw in Chapter One that that's not true. And others such as Sidgwick reject psychological hedonism, recognizing that we can want many other things. This has an important implication.

If all you could want was your own pleasure, all that could be good from your point of view—because it would be all you could seek—would be your own pleasure; other people's could have no worth. But if we separate ethical from psychological hedonism, the former needn't take this egoistic form. It can say that what's good is *everyone's* pleasure, so you ought to pursue the most good feeling for everyone, which can mean giving up a lesser pleasure for yourself to give a greater one to someone else. This connects hedonism not to selfishness but to altruism, but what the altruism aims at is still just pleasure and the absence of pain—what's good in others' lives as well as your own is just good feeling.

Even in this altruistic form, however, ethical hedonism is too narrow to be credible. There are two main arguments why pleasure isn't the only good.

The first argument concerns morally vicious pleasures. Imagine that a torturer is inflicting intense pain on a victim and taking pleasure in doing so. He's a sadist, delighting both in the pain he's causing his victim and in the fact that he's causing it. According to hedonism, his sadistic pleasure makes the situation better than if he had no feelings about his victim's pain or, worse, were pained by it. Since it's pleasant, it's a good. His pleasure may have bad effects on other people if it makes him torture more energetically now or more likely to torture in the future; then it's bad as a means. But in itself his pleasure is by hedonist standards good, and it will be purely good if it doesn't have those effects. If he's already torturing as much as he can (his machine is already set to the maximum) and he won't torture again (this is his last day on the job), his sadistic pleasure has only positive value.

This is hard to accept, for surely the torturer's pleasure makes the situation worse. Even if it's to some degree good because it's pleasant—itself a controversial claim—it's also bad because it's sadistic, and more bad than it is good. Its bad aspect outweighs any good it may contain, so on balance it's undesirable. Even apart from any further effects, a world with a gleeful torturer is worse than one with a reluctant torturer, and the torturer's life is also worse. It's less good for him to thrill at others' pain than not to, even if the thrilling gives him joy.

Nor is this true only of extreme vices such as sadism. If someone you dislike doesn't get a job he wanted, you may take a mild malicious pleasure in his failure. Your pleasure may be to some degree good as a pleasure, but it's also evil because it's malicious, and probably evil on balance. Your life would be better without that nasty joy.

Or consider virtuous pains, as when you see the torturer at work and feel pained by his victim's pain. Though you can't do anything to stop the victim's pain, you sympathize with her and hurt for her hurt. Ethical hedonism says your compassionate pain only makes the situation worse—it would be better if you were unmoved—and that's again hard to accept. Compassion is a morally fitting response to another's pain, and because it's fitting, it's good. Compassionate pain may also be bad as pain—maybe any pain is bad insofar as it's pain—but it's also good insofar as it's compassionate, and overall usually more good than bad. On balance it's better to feel for others' troubles than to be callously indifferent to them.

Or imagine two worlds containing equal amounts of pleasure. In the first world everyone is selfish. They take no pleasure in each other's pleasure and make no effort to promote it; each cares only about himself. But people in the second world are benevolent, helping each other to be happy and delighting when they are happy. Isn't the second world better?

It may be said the two worlds can't contain equal pleasure: given how they benefit each other, people in the second world will be happier than in the first. But the advantage deriving from their virtue can be exactly cancelled by greater natural advantages in the first world, such as warmer weather and less disease. If the result is that the two worlds are equally happy, hedonism says they're equally good. But if we could bring just one of them into existence, wouldn't we prefer the second?

These arguments suggest that not only pleasure but also virtue—having morally fitting feelings and desires—is good, while vice as well as pain is evil. Both the world and your life will be better if you care benevolently for others than if you maliciously try to hurt them, and that can be true even if your virtue means you end up feeling less pleasure than you might.

Certainly many philosophers have thought this. Socrates, Plato, and Aristotle all believed that moral virtue is an essential element in a good life, with Socrates saying it's better to be a just or virtuous person who suffers than an unjust one who's happy. But even if we don't share that extreme view, we should add virtue to pleasure as one item on the list of ultimate goods. And there's a second argument against hedonism, pointing to a second category of further goods.

MINDLESS PLEASURES

This argument concerns mindless pleasures, ones that though not morally vicious don't involve anything else that could have value: no exercise of intelligence, no creativity, no love or achievement. Hedonism says a life containing only these pleasures could be supremely good, and that's again hard to accept.

This argument appears often in literature. Early in the *Odyssey*, Odysseus and his men visit the lotus-eaters, who spend their days eating the fruit of a narcotic plant and drowsing contentedly; though extremely pleasant, their life is presented as a temptation Odysseus should resist. (He does, though some of his men do not.) In *Brave New World*, the lower orders, the deltas and epsilons, take a similarly pleasurable drug called soma, watch "feelies," and have frequent recreational sex. This makes their lives highly enjoyable: they're being accurate when they say, "Everyone's happy here." But most readers don't find the novel's world ideal; we think its characters' lives are deeply impoverished by their lack of control over their existence. They've been bred to want only passive pleasure, not understanding or real achievement. They don't do or know anything; they just feel. And feeling isn't enough.

In a philosopher's version of this argument, Robert Nozick asks us to imagine an "experience machine" that by electrically stimulating your brain can give you the experience and therefore the pleasure of anything you like. Before you plug in, you decide what feelings you'd like to have—of being the first person to climb Mount Everest, of making a major scientific discovery, of seducing Brad Pitt. And it's then just as if you were doing those things: it feels exactly as if you were climbing Everest, discovering gravity, or seducing Brad, and gives you all the same pleasure.

Your pleasures on the experience machine needn't be mindless in the same way as those of eating lotus or watching feelies. They can be ones that normally accompany challenging activities such as climbing mountains and performing scientific experiments. But since you're not actually doing those things, you don't actually face any challenge. That's why for many of us a whole life on the machine wouldn't, for all its pleasures, be very good. If you chose it over even a moderately enjoyable life of the kind most of us lead, you'd be choosing something less good. An experience machine might be fun for an occasional evening's entertainment; maybe we use TV and movies as substitute experience machines. But for many of us a whole life of only good feeling would lack important human goods.

What are these goods? At one point Nozick suggests that we can't have a character on the experience machine. We want to *be* a certain way—say, courageous or compassionate—and there's no way we *are* while being fed experiences. But this needn't be true. You can take your character with you onto the machine and let it determine how you respond there; if you're compassionate, you'll respond with sympathy to seeing others hurt. You can even use your knowledge of your character to guide your selection of experiences. If you're a little cowardly, you won't choose experiences that seem to pose dangers; if you like thrills, you will.

You can even use the machine to improve your character. You can program it to give you a sequence of experiences through which you'll become more courageous or compassionate, and make the change more quickly than you could in real life. So it's not character as such that's missing.

Another idea of Nozick's is that the experience machine cuts us off from contact with any deeper reality, such as can be found in mystical religious experience or perhaps through psychedelic drugs. But we needn't believe in a deeper reality to find life on the machine less than ideal. Nozick is closer to the mark when he says the machine cuts us off from contact with reality more generally, including the everyday reality of our surroundings. We normally live within a physical world, related to and in constant interaction with it. But the machine severs our connection to this world, in three ways.

First, while on it you don't have knowledge of the world around you and your place in it. You think you're climbing Everest or discovering gravity, but in fact you're sitting motionless with electrodes attached to your brain. Your beliefs about your situation therefore don't match what that situation is, as true beliefs or knowledge would; they're completely inaccurate. Second, you don't actually achieve any goals on the machine. You want to make it the case that you've climbed Everest or discovered gravity, but you don't really do those things. And that means another relation to reality is missing: when you formulate a goal in your mind and then change the world to match it. That's genuine achievement, which you also lack on the machine. Nor, finally, do you have real relations with other people. You don't know an actual person's character or have real effects on her life, nor do you love someone who loves you back. Just as you're not in genuine contact with your physical surroundings, so you're not in genuine contact with other people. You're isolated within your mind, having only internal experiences that aren't connected to what's outside you.

This is also the situation in the movie *The Matrix*. There ordinary life is the illusion, created for the movie's characters by machines who use human bodies as energy sources. And reality, for those who escape the illusion, is grim: living in cramped quarters with boring food and few opportunities for enjoyment, they have to constantly fight the machines.

Again there's a choice between more pleasure—though now just the limited pleasures of everyday life—and contact with reality. And the movie, through its hero, Neo, prefers the contact.

That said, *The Matrix* is less hostile to the contrary choice than Nozick or *Brave New World* is. When another character, Cypher, abandons reality and returns to the comfort of the matrix, his decision is presented as at least understandable. But in the context of *The Matrix*, there's a reason why that's so.

Earlier in this chapter I said the value of increases in your pleasure becomes less the more pleasure you have. (This was the flattening curve in Figure 3.1.) But then the boost in pleasure the matrix illusion gives (from something very grim to the feelings of everyday life) has more value than that from the experience machine (from everyday life to something even more enjoyable). And a loss of contact with reality that clearly outweighs the second boost may not so decisively outweigh the first. In any case, it would be wrong to conclude from Nozick's example that pleasure has no value. It remains one good among others and can sometimes be the most important. If you had to choose between a pleasant illusion and a reality of unrelenting agony, the illusion would surely be best.

Virtue is often called a moral good, while knowledge and achievement are non-moral, but they too have been endorsed by philosophers. Plato and Aristotle thought knowledge the greatest good of all, more important even than moral virtue, as did St. Thomas Aquinas and G. W. F. Hegel. Marx and Nietzsche prized achievement, or successfully willing changes in the world. Even John Stuart Mill, a utilitarian but not a consistent hedonist, said it's better to be a human being dissatisfied than a pig satisfied, or Socrates dissatisfied than a fool satisfied.

Some philosophers have tied these goods to our distinctive nature as humans. Pleasure, they've said, is something animals too can feel; it's therefore a lower and even bestial value. Only in developing our distinctive capacities such as rationality can our true good be found.

As I argued earlier, this appeal to distinctive capacities is dangerous. If we learn that dolphins or some aliens can reason just like us, will that mean our doing so is no longer good? And the appeal doesn't fit our current argument. Many pleasures you have on the experience machine are distinctively human; other animals can't be pleased to be the first up a mountain or to have discovered gravity. And a key part of what's missing on the machine isn't distinctive. Animals too can be in contact with reality: they too can have some knowledge of their surroundings and achieve some goals, such as to catch and eat this prey.

It's far better to value knowledge, achievement, and real human relations just as such, regardless of whether other beings share them. These goods connect states of our mind, often ones formed using rationality, to aspects of the outside world, and that's enough to give them value.

So there are two arguments why pleasure and pain aren't the only intrinsic values. The first concerns morally vicious pleasures, such as malicious pleasures, and virtuous pains, such as those of compassion; the second concerns mindless pleasures, which involve no exercise of intelligence or contact with reality. The first argument points to an additional good of virtue and evil of vice, the second to goods that relate us to the world, such as knowledge and achievement.

In the next few chapters we'll examine these goods, beginning with those that relate us to the world. There will be a chapter on knowledge, one on achievement, and then—switching to the other category—a chapter on virtue. That will lead to a discussion of love and friendship as embodying all these goods plus pleasure at once.

FURTHER READINGS

The idea that pleasure is less good than pain is evil is defended most fully in Jamie Mayerfeld, *Suffering and Moral Responsibility*, chap. 6. Derek Parfit discusses our attitude to past pleasures and pains in *Reasons and Persons*, chap. 8, while T. H. Green's argument that pleasure can't be good because it doesn't provide "abiding satisfaction" occurs in his *Prolegomena to Ethics*, bk. 3, chap. 4. The objection that ethical hedonism finds malicious pleasures purely good is made by, among others, C. D. Broad in *Five Types of Ethical Theory*. Robert Nozick discusses the "experience machine" in *Anarchy, State, and Utopia*, chap. 3, and again in *The Examined Life*, chap. 10; John Stuart Mill's comment about the human and the pig is in his *Utilitarianism*, chap. 2.

Chapter Four

KNOWING WHAT'S WHAT

I gotta know, gotta know, gotta know . . .

—Elvis Presley

One kind of contact that's missing on the experience machine is knowledge, of the world and of your place in it. If that's a bad thing, then knowledge must be good. And much that we do shows that we believe this.

Why do we educate our children? Partly to give them skills so they can find jobs in later life, but also because we think it's good in itself to know something about the laws of nature and the history of your culture. Our schools don't teach only what's practical. If we become experts on some topic, even just gardening or a favorite rock band, we feel proud of that fact. And if we ask about humanity's greatest achievements, surely one is our knowledge of the universe. A physicist can know about events 13.7 billion years ago, just after the big bang, and about objects 45 billion light-years away. Isn't that impressive? Space research has brought us technological benefits (the Teflon frying pan!) but has been justified far more by what it's helped us learn.

What exactly is knowledge? When you know something you have a picture of the world that matches the way the world is, so things are as you represent them to be. You believe it's raining and it is, or you think stegosauruses lived in the Jurassic period and they did. Knowing involves believing something true, and that's a large part of its value, giving you a tie to reality that's missing on the experience machine.

But knowledge involves more. If you think it will rain tomorrow despite reading several forecasts of sun, then even if it does rain you didn't know it would, because your belief was true only by luck. To know something you need a belief about it that's justified by your evidence, or that you reached by means that normally lead to truth; you need a belief that both is true and should be true given how you acquired it, and the second condition makes for an even tighter tie to reality. Not only does your mind match the world as it is now, but it probably also would have matched it if things were different, because then too you would have based your belief on evidence.

Not all knowledge is equally worth having, though. Knowing a law of nature is significantly good apart from any further benefits it brings; so is understanding a close friend's character. But knowing the number of blades of grass on your lawn isn't. If you took the trouble to learn that—if you spent the requisite hours on your knees counting—the resulting value (if any) wouldn't justify your effort: that kind of knowledge is trivial.

So some kinds of knowledge are better than others, and there must be features that make them so. In this chapter I'll try to identify these features, or determine which truths are more worth knowing and why.

Here it will help to divide knowledge into three categories. The first involves knowing the world outside you, apart from any relations between it and you. It includes knowing general laws of nature and also particular facts such as that it's raining in Toronto now. Both of these would be true even if you didn't exist, so in knowing them you know an entirely independent reality.

The second category is knowledge of your relation to the world, or how you're placed in it. It includes knowing where you are in space, such as climbing Everest or sitting at a desk, and how you relate to other people: that some are looking at you now or that others find you annoying.

The final category is knowledge of your own internal states, both particular thoughts or feelings and lasting traits of character. Thus you can know that you're tasting an orange now or that you tend to envy your friends' successes.

Let's start with the first category.

KNOWING THE WORLD

Philosophers who've discussed the value of knowledge have mostly had in mind the first kind, that of the outside world. But their ideal for this knowledge hasn't involved knowing particular external facts such as the weather now or the number of blades of grass in a lawn. Instead they've emphasized knowing more general or explanatory truths such as scientific laws or, if there are any, the truths of metaphysics. They've valued fundamental rather than incidental knowledge, the kind had by scientists and philosophers rather than trivia buffs. And this seems right: if it's good to know external reality, it seems especially good to know general truths about it. But there are two ways a truth can be general.

In one sense, a truth is general if its content is widely extended: if it concerns a large part of the world or a great many objects in it. In this sense a truth about the grass on your lawn isn't very general; it concerns just a small area in space at a particular time. But a scientific law applies to a huge number of objects at many places and times. The law of falling bodies on earth governs all physical objects near the earth throughout its history, so it's far more extended than a truth about your lawn. More fundamental laws such as the law of gravity are even more wide-ranging, applying out to the edges of the universe. And if there are truths of metaphysics, they apply to non-physical objects as well as to objects in possible universes with different laws than our own; this is one reason why some philosophers have thought metaphysical knowledge the best knowledge there is.

An ideal of extended knowledge fits the initial rationale for valuing knowledge. If knowing involves matching your mind to reality, you do so to a higher degree if you match more of reality by knowing a truth that applies to more of it. Knowing the number of blades of grass in your lawn relates your mind to just a small piece of the world; knowing about gravity connects you to an aspect of the whole thing.

Extended knowledge is also something only we humans can have. (This doesn't make such knowledge good, but it helps explain why our lives can be better than other animals'.)

A dog can believe and maybe know that its master has come home, but it can't form explicit generalizations about what its master always does, and it certainly can't know truths as extended as the law of gravity.

But the extent of its content isn't the only thing that makes a truth more worth knowing. There's another sense of generality that partly overlaps with the first one and partly is distinct.

In this second sense, generality means explanatory importance, so an item of knowledge is general if you've used it to explain a great many other things you know. If you know the law of gravity, you can use it to explain more specific laws like the one about falling bodies on earth: given that law plus facts such as the earth's mass, those bodies have to accelerate at 9.8 m/sec^2. And you can use the more specific law to explain many particular facts. That falling objects accelerate at 9.8 m/sec^2 explains why a ball dropped two seconds ago is falling at 19.6 m/sec, and that truth, combined with others about the ball's mass and the molecular structure of glass, explains why a window will break if the ball hits it.

These nested explanations, some explained by others, can organize the things you know in a hierarchy, with items higher up in the hierarchy explaining ones lower down, as in Figure 4.1. Here each circle represents a truth you know, with the slanted lines showing when you've used one truth to explain another. Thus you've used your knowledge of the top truth to explain the two below it—maybe the top one is the law of gravity and the others are more specific laws of motion—and each of them to explain two further facts. The idea is that items of knowledge are more general, and therefore more valuable, when they've been used to explain more other truths, so they have more items below them in this kind of hierarchy.

Though we can't measure explanatory generality precisely, here is one way it could in principle be done. We give each point in the hierarchy one unit of value for being an item of knowledge and then an extra unit for every other item below it, or every other truth it's been used to explain. Then the bottom four points in Figure 4.1 each have one unit of value, the two above them have three units (their own plus one for each of the two below them), and the top point has seven. This makes for a total of seventeen units of value in the hierarchy as a whole, which is more than the seven units there would be if you knew seven unconnected truths. Making explanatory connections between things you know increases the value of your knowledge, in particular by increasing the value of its most explanatory elements.

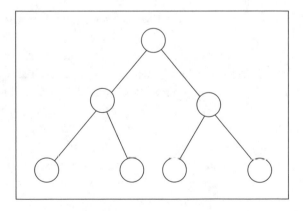

Figure 4.1

Knowing the number of blades of grass in a lawn isn't general in this sense either, because it doesn't explain anything. It's trivial not only because it's localized in its subject matter but also because it illuminates nothing else. (It could figure in an explanatory hierarchy if it was explained by other truths, for example laws about how grass grows. But then it would be those other truths that had extra value.) Knowing scientific laws, by contrast, can be and often is explanatorily general. Precisely because they apply to so many objects, they can explain many individual phenomena.

Consider the grand unified theory sought by physicists, which would reduce the four basic physical forces, including gravity, to a single fundamental one. A law governing this one fundamental force would be immensely extended, applying to every material thing in the universe, and it would also have tremendous explanatory power. Each of the four forces already explains a great deal; a truth that explained them all would gather all their hierarchies below it and be immensely general.

Explanatory generality was also behind Aquinas's view that the best knowledge is knowledge of God. Aquinas didn't argue, as some have, that knowing God is best because he's the best thing in the universe, and the best knowledge must have the best object. Instead, he said God is the First Cause of the universe and therefore responsible for every created effect: to know him is potentially to know the explanation of everything else.

Philosophers have said the same about their favorite, metaphysical knowledge: if there are truths about what all beings are like just as beings, they're immensely explanatory. (Of course it's fishy: philosophers philosophizing that philosophers' knowledge is best. But think of it as like those pop songs that extol their own style of music as best: "It don't mean a thing if it ain't got that swing" or "It's gotta be rock and roll music"— biased but harmless.) Certainly if there is metaphysical knowledge, it has both of the traits that make knowledge most worth having.

The two kinds of generality therefore often overlap, but they don't do so always. You can know an extended law but not have used it to explain much else; for example, you haven't combined it with truths about particular objects to explain their speeds right now. Then your knowledge is general in the first sense but not in the second. Conversely, most explanations combine an extended truth with more particular ones, say, about when an object was dropped, and if one of these truths figures in many explanations, it can be general in the second sense but not the first. This happens often in subjects like history and psychology. There a particular truth about a crucial political event or a trauma in a person's childhood can explain many subsequent events without itself being very extended. Despite being very local, a truth about a key military battle or presidential election can powerfully influence a nation's later history and so have great explanatory importance.

However it relates to extent, to value explanatory generality is really to value understanding, where you not only know *that* something is the case but also know *why* it's the case. You understand a truth when you can place it in a larger context and connect it to more fundamental principles that explain why it holds. That connection and the understanding it leads to are precisely what generality in the explanatory sense finds good, and the idea that they're good is again intuitive. To match your mind to the world you have to match not only the separate facts it contains but also the explanatory relations between them. If you know only what's true but not why, you don't know everything there is to know because you don't know what accounts for what. And the capacity to know this again distinguishes us from other animals. Maybe a dog can know that a ball is falling, but it can't understand why it's falling by connecting that fact to more abstract truths about why bodies in general fall.

In its best, top-to-bottom form, understanding combines two distinct intellectual styles that have been associated with the cities of Athens and Manchester. Athenian knowledge is of highly abstract principles such as those known by a theoretical physicist; that of Manchester (home of the industrial revolution) concerns a great many particular facts, such as those known to a biologist studying a particular swamp or forest. The best understanding combines the two, so you both know abstract principles and know many particular facts that you use the principles to explain: while the principles give unity to your beliefs, the facts add substance. The Athenian and Mancunian styles may appeal to different people: some may prefer to reflect on timeless abstract truths, others to amass reams of particular data. But the best understanding would incorporate them both.

While this understanding is sought by scientists, philosophers, and other intellectuals, something similar can be had on more everyday topics. Let's say you know how a friend reacts to situations and why. He bristles at criticism, for example, because he lacks self-confidence, owing to some embarrassing failures in his past. None of what you know about him is as extended as the law of gravity, but it's nonetheless organized in a hierarchy with many particular truths explained by more general ones about his personality and history. On a less grandiose topic, it's still integrated knowledge.

Or maybe you're a car mechanic who knows what makes engines run, what the signs of different problems in them are, and how best to fix those problems. Your knowledge again involves complex relations among different truths, amounting to an understanding of engines and their repair. Or you have organized beliefs about gardening, hockey, or making jam. Explanatory generality isn't found only in abstruse intellectual knowledge, but can be achieved to some degree in many fields. Philosophers haven't always emphasized this, concentrating too much on abstract understanding and making the value of knowledge seem esoteric and elitist. But it's a partly populist value, open to a significant degree to us all.

The explanatory ideal has further aspects. Imagine that you've used the law of falling bodies to explain the speeds of a hundred different dropped objects. Though valuable, your knowledge isn't terribly exciting, because the truths you've explained are so similar. It would be more impressive to use a single law to explain what initially seemed to be unconnected facts, so you make surprising connections between them. This was a key merit of Newton's laws: they showed how motions people had thought were unrelated—of objects on Earth and in the heavens—followed the same principles. And we can recognize this merit by making a truth's explanatory generality depend not just on how many individual truths it explains but also on how many different *kinds* of truth it explains. Then the top item in Figure 4.1 has more value if the two below it concern different subjects;

likewise, each of those two counts more if it explains different kinds of fact. More varied hierarchies of truths are better, and the most impressive understanding unites disparate phenomena.

The ideal also values precise knowledge. You can know that objects accelerate toward the earth at 9.8 m/sec^2 or know only that they accelerate at somewhere between 7 and 13 m/sec^2. In the first case you know a greater number of individual truths: you know not only that objects accelerate between at 7 and 13 m/sec^2, but also that they do so at between 8 and 12, 9 and 11, and so on. And you can therefore explain more truths: not only why the speed of an object dropped two seconds ago is between 14 and 26 m/sec, but also why it's within ever narrower bands. The extra truths you've explained are similar to each other, so you don't here have the extra value of varied explanation. But the simple number of truths explained remains one aspect of explanatory generality, and it's surely right that more precise knowledge is better. When you know specific rather than vague facts, you both know and can explain more about the world.

These further aspects of the explanatory ideal can again be found on everyday topics. Your understanding of a friend can encompass his athletic abilities, emotional responses, and sense of humor— all very different—while giving them a partly common explanation in aspects of his history; you can also know exactly what kind of music he likes or what specific gesture will cheer him up. A mechanic's knowledge can combine different subject matters—carburetors, gearboxes, tires— and make precise discriminations about each. The full cognitive ideal is well-justified true belief that's precise and explains many other truths of different kinds. While this may be found to the highest degree in scientific knowledge, it's also possible on less grand topics.

KNOWING YOUR PLACE

So far we've discussed knowledge of the outside world, especially of general truths about it, and you can lack this on the experience machine. You can believe in scientific laws that fit your experiences there but don't fit reality, so your beliefs aren't true of reality. Or you can have scientific beliefs that, though true, weren't acquired in the way required for knowledge.

But neither of these need be so. You can program a world with the same laws as ours and take your existing scientific beliefs with you onto the machine; if they were knowledge before you plugged in, they will be after. In any case, a lack of scientific knowledge doesn't seem the most troubling thing about your cognitive state on the machine. Far more salient is your lack of another kind of knowledge.

This is knowledge of the second kind, of your relation to things in the world. And here you not only lack knowledge but also have positively false beliefs. You think you're climbing Everest or discovering gravity when you're in fact sitting motionless with electrodes attached to your brain. Instead of a match with reality, there's a positive mismatch, or a representation of your place in the world that's false.

This is a key feature of the machine and seems to do more to make your condition there less good than any lack of scientific understanding; it's these errors about your immediate situation that matter most. Why? The truths you don't know aren't general in either of our two senses. That you're at a particular place in the world isn't an extended truth—it concerns only you and that place now. Nor does it explain much—it has no large hierarchy of other truths below it. But being right rather than wrong about it does seem very important, and the same holds for some other truths in this category.

Imagine you're contented with some aspects of your life. You believe your wife is faithful to you and take pleasure in that belief; you also think your colleagues at work admire you, and you're pleased by that. But both beliefs are false: your wife has multiple lovers, and your colleagues ridicule you behind your back.

If pleasure alone were good, your condition here would be ideal, since you have only pleasant feelings. But surely your delusions make your life worse—it's bad to be deceived in these matters. And the beliefs are again in our second category. Though not especially general, they concern your relation to the world around you and, more specifically, to people who are important in your life. Though your ignorance is bliss, this bliss isn't best.

Not all knowledge in the second category has this importance. If you're wrong about how many miles you are from Mumbai, that's not a serious blight on your life. Nor does it matter much if you believe falsely that some distant person you'll never meet respects you. It's knowing about your relations to your immediate environment and to people you're in regular contact with that has special value.

We may be able to explain why. Knowledge is good as an instance of connection to reality, but the truths we're now concerned with are themselves about that connection: they're about where you are in space and how you relate to things around you. And the value of contact with reality may be especially realized in knowing about your own contact, so it's especially important to be tied to your tie to your environment. On the experience machine your mind in one sense floats free, since its contents are whatever you chose them to be. But in another sense it's connected to a particular body in a particular location and influenced by what happens there. Having accurate beliefs about that connection—being properly connected to it—may therefore have special importance.

A question remains, though, about the kind of importance this is. Your condition on the experience machine could be less than ideal because, though containing only intrinsic goods such as pleasure, it lacks other goods such as knowledge. Or it could be that, while containing pleasure, it also contains significant evils that weigh against it, so it not only lacks positive values but includes negative ones. Just as pain is the contrary of pleasure, so false belief is the contrary of knowledge and can therefore be evil. Do your mistaken beliefs on the machine about where you are involve mainly the absence of a good of knowledge or the presence of an evil of error?

To me they involve mainly the presence of an evil, and the reason is just that the knowledge considered on its own isn't significantly good. If you're nearing the end of a painful terminal illness, there are goods that can make your continuing to live worthwhile: maybe you'll complete a lifelong project or have loving interactions with friends. At the end of his life, Freud refused painkillers so he could keep thinking clearly; given the quality of his thinking, that was a reasonable choice.

But imagine that the good to be weighed against your pain is just your knowing that you're now lying in a hospital bed. That seems to have little weight against the pain and to supply little reason for you to suffer through it. Given its limited generality, it isn't very valuable, and the same is true of other beliefs of this kind. If we ask what gives our everyday lives value, the fact that we know where we are isn't a large part of the answer, nor is it a great good to know whether your wife is faithful or what your co-workers think about you.

But then if the difference between having true and false beliefs on these topics is as important as I've said, it must be because the false beliefs are significantly evil, and that does seem right. Being positively mistaken about where you are or how you relate to people near you is an important evil even though knowing these things isn't an important good; the mismatch is a greater evil than the match is a good. Earlier I argued that pain is more evil than pleasure is good, and there's a similar asymmetry here. Being wrong about some truths in our second category is more evil than knowing them is good; with these truths it's more important to avoid the evil of error than to achieve any good in getting them right.

Interestingly, this asymmetry seems not to apply to truths about the outside world. Consider a scientist of the past who had false beliefs about the laws of nature: for example, Aristotle in his role as a physicist, where he proposed laws of motion that were later disproved by Galileo. Were these false beliefs of Aristotle's significantly evil, and did they make his state of mind worse than that of his contemporaries who had no beliefs about these laws? That doesn't seem right. While it would have been good for Aristotle to have true scientific beliefs, it wasn't significantly bad or even bad at all that he had false ones, and it certainly wasn't worse than if he'd had no scientific beliefs. So in this case the asymmetry runs in the opposite direction. Knowledge in the first category can be significantly good, and in particular is more good than false belief about the same topics is evil; here the tendency is to accentuate the positive.

But the same isn't true of knowledge in the second category, at least when it concerns your immediate surroundings: there false belief is more evil than knowledge is good. It's vital to know where you are in the world, or to be properly connected to facts about how you relate to your environment, and the fact that you're not so connected is one reason why life on the experience machine isn't best. But the reason isn't that knowing these truths is a great intrinsic good; it's that being wrong about them is a great evil.

KNOWING YOURSELF

The final category of knowledge is of your inner states: your thoughts, feelings, and traits of character. Unlike the other two, this knowledge isn't seriously threatened on the experience machine. Even when you're plugged in, you can know what you're thinking now, and though you lack some evidence about your character—you can't see how real people react to you—you can learn as much about it by introspection as you could in ordinary life.

This kind of knowledge certainly has value, especially if it's general in our two senses. Just as knowledge of a friend is good when it's arranged in an explanatory hierarchy, so is self-knowledge. As a boy I noticed that I was bad at chess, reading maps on canoe trips, and judging bounces off the boards in hockey, but I saw no connection between the three. Later I learned that there's a distinct spatial intelligence, involving the ability to process spatial information, and that my failings all turned on my not having much of that. Here I'd unified several truths under a single explanatory one and come to understand them; just as that would've been good about another person, so it was good about me.

But self-knowledge has often been thought specially important just because it's self-knowledge. In ancient Greece the Delphic oracle's main advice was "Know thyself," while psychiatric programs such as Freudianism offer a journey toward self-discovery. Both treat self-knowledge as vitally important because it's about you.

One basis for this view is the effects of self-knowledge. If you have a talent for business but none for singing, it's a mistake—it won't give you a happy or successful life—to pursue a career in opera rather than start a company. If you want to improve your moral character, you first need to know what it is now and where it's flawed. These instrumental points may be enough to explain the interest in self-knowledge of Greek oracles and twentieth-century psychiatrists—they saw it as a means to a life that's on other grounds good.

But self-knowledge can also be harmful, and sometimes it's self-delusion that's beneficial. Just as falsely believing that others respect you can make you happy, so can having an inflated opinion of your talents or virtues. And exaggerating your merits can stimulate other goods such as achievement.

We're certainly prone to this exaggeration. In one survey, 88 percent of American college students said they were better-than-average drivers—mathematically impossible, but what they believed. In another, 94 percent of professors (94 percent!) said their scholarship was above average. Psychologists call this the "Lake Wobegon effect," after the fictional Minnesota town where all the children are above average, and it's utterly pervasive. Studies show that stockbrokers, police officers, musicians, carpenters, and others all think they're better than average and therefore better than they really are.

Though there's self-delusion here, it can prompt us to achieve more than we otherwise would. If you're a professor and believe your scholarship is just average, how hard will you work at it? Not very hard, I suspect. But if you believe falsely that it's better than other people's, won't you put more effort into it and therefore produce better scholarship? If so, your false belief about yourself will boost your performance, and the same holds in other fields. If you think you're in the top 10 percent for guitar talent, you'll practice a certain amount; if you believe mistakenly that you're in the top 1 percent, you'll practice harder and end up playing better. You'll make more of your talents if you think they're greater than they are.

This is one reason why, as Robert Browning said, "a man's reach should exceed his grasp." If you reach for more than you can actually grasp, you'll end up grasping more than if you'd reached for less. But doing that requires believing that your reach extends further than it does.

So self-knowledge can be limiting as well as beneficial—it can hinder rather than promote other goods. But our question is whether it has special value in itself, or apart from its effects. Is self-knowledge distinctively important because it's of the self?

We can imagine an argument that it is. The value of knowing external reality depends only on its generality, but knowing your relation to the world has extra value because it's partly about you. But then knowing your internal states, which are only about you, should have even greater value. Alexander Pope wrote, "The proper study of mankind is man"; by extension, for any particular person the proper study of her is her.

I'm not persuaded by this argument. Self-knowledge is hard to evaluate because of its many cross-cutting effects, but I don't think it has anything like the intrinsic importance of knowing your place in the world.

If your false beliefs about your situation on the experience machine make you happy, that doesn't stop them from being seriously regrettable because they're false, and the same holds if errors in the second category promote other goods. Maybe believing falsely that your colleagues respect you will make you work harder and achieve more; even so, being wrong about your relations to people close to you is significantly bad. But if exaggerating your talents makes you achieve more, the mistake doesn't seem to me so bad; if it really does promote achievement, that's surely the vital thing. If we'd all accomplish more by exaggerating our talents, shouldn't we all just exaggerate?

The same holds for more particular items of inner knowledge. In Chapter Two I suggested that in a flow experience you may feel pleasure but not entirely notice it. This may be unfortunate if being aware of the pleasure would heighten it and allow you a further pleasure-that in the fact that you're feeling it. But these effects aside, how good is it to know that you're having a particular feeling? I just don't see it as that important. When you look back on a flow experience, do you wish you'd attended more to the thrill, just so you could have known about it? I don't think so. The main thing is that the thrill was there.

So I don't think knowledge has more intrinsic value the more it's about you. Instead, the two non-relational types of knowledge—just about the outside world or just about you— have value that depends only on their generality, while some knowledge that mixes the two, because it's about your relation to your immediate environment, has extra value. And that, I've suggested, may be because the value of being connected to reality is especially realized in knowing about that connection.

This doesn't mean self-knowledge has no value: understanding yourself remains as good as understanding other people or things. And sometimes it's hugely beneficial, as when it helps you choose a rewarding career or improve your character. But its effects aside, self-knowledge doesn't seem so special: it has neither the generality of scientific knowledge nor the extra importance of knowing your place in the world. While it's good to know your inner states, it's no tragedy if you don't, and if being wrong about them helps you achieve other important goods, that's probably on balance a blessing.

MORAL KNOWLEDGE

There's another kind of knowledge to consider: moral knowledge, or knowing what's right and wrong or good and bad. It's the knowledge moral philosophers seek and that you may gain some of by reading this book. How important is it as a kind of knowledge?

Philosophers have again rated this knowledge highly, and it can certainly have desirable effects: if you know what's truly good, you're more likely to seek it and to avoid what's bad. Moral knowledge can also be good in itself if it's general. The belief that pleasure is good, for example, is reasonably extended, since it applies to all pleasant experiences, and it's also explanatory since it explains of each such experience why it's good. And moral beliefs can be arranged in hierarchies. You can first believe that knowledge and achievement are good, and then unify those beliefs by seeing the two as forms of a more abstract good of contact with reality. That unifies diverse values in the same way Newton's laws unified motions on earth and in the heavens.

But I again don't see that moral knowledge has the extra intrinsic value some philosophers have claimed. Why should knowing what's good or right be specially important as a form of knowing? Why should it be more important in itself to be right about those kinds of truth than about others? If anything, there are limits on the value of moral knowledge. The truths that figure in a moral hierarchy are all of the same broad kind—they're all about what's good or right—so there can't be the wide variety of explained truths found in the best scientific understanding. And the hierarchy can't have that many levels, since there aren't that many distinct moral principles—the complexity of moral understanding only goes so far.

So if reading this book increases your moral knowledge, that will be a good thing apart from its effects. But it won't be the best possible thing, or make for the greatest possible increase in the value of your beliefs. There are many valuable forms of knowledge, or ways of having your mind match reality, and moral knowledge is one of them. But it isn't a uniquely valuable form of knowledge; while moral facts are good to know, so are many other kinds of fact. That's been a key thesis of this chapter: that the value of knowledge, while largely missing on the experience machine, can be found on many topics and by many different people—not just scientists and philosophers, but also friends, car mechanics, and gardeners. Far from the elitist value some philosophers have described, it's one that's available to some degree to us all.

FURTHER READINGS

The idea that philosophical knowledge is best is affirmed by Socrates in Plato's *Apology*, Aristotle in *Nicomachean Ethics*, bk. 10, and G. W. F. Hegel in *The Phenomenology of Spirit*; claims about the value of specifically metaphysical and moral knowledge are in Hastings Rashdall, *The Theory of Good and Evil*, vol. 2, chap. 5. The idea that the value of an item of knowledge depends on its generality is defended in W. D. Ross, *The Right and the Good*, chap. 6, and at greater length in my *Perfectionism*, chaps. 8–10. The example of being deceived about your wife and colleagues is modeled on one in Thomas Nagel's "Death."

Chapter Five

MAKING THINGS HAPPEN

If I could change the world . . .

—Eric Clapton

The second good of connection to reality is achievement. Like knowledge, it involves a match between your mind and the world, but now running in the opposite direction. In knowledge you take the world as given and fit your mind to it: if it's raining, you come to believe that it's raining. But in achievement you first form a goal in your mind (a more equal division of incomes in your country or yourself on top of Everest) and then realize it (you equalize incomes or climb the mountain). The result is again a correspondence between something in your mind and part of the world, but instead of fitting your mind to the world, you've made the world fit your mind. You've mastered reality by imposing an idea on it.

Not every effect you have involves this mastery. To transfer an idea to reality you have to have the idea in the first place: you have to intend to produce some goal and then do so. But many changes you make don't involve this process. When you breathe, you move air molecules around you and create sound waves, but since you don't intend these results, they aren't things you achieve. They don't impose your will on the world because they don't involve your will at all.

Like knowledge, achievement is something missing on the experience machine. You form goals there and believe you're realizing them, but you're not; you're not really climbing Everest or discovering gravity. And that lack of willed impact on the world is a key reason why life on the machine isn't best. You don't actually accomplish anything there, in the sense of intending and effecting real change.

Again like knowledge, achievement involves more than just a match with reality. To know it will rain tomorrow you have to have arrived at that belief in a way that made its being true not a fluke. Likewise, to have its full value, your achieving a goal can't be a matter of luck. You have to have pursued the goal intelligently, or in a way that, given what you knew beforehand, made your succeeding likely. You can't have sought a more equal division of incomes by means that had little chance of producing it but then somehow, by chance, did.

Achievement often has instrumental value. If you successfully pursue a good goal such as a friend's happiness, your doing so is good as a means or because it produces happiness, and that may be the most important thing about it. But your achievement is also good in itself, or as part of your life. If your friend got the same happiness independently of you, that would be just as great a good in her life. She would be just as happy, which would have just as much value. But it wouldn't be as good in *your* life. It makes your life better if *you* sought and produced that happiness rather than watching it happen; then you willed that effect. So even when it produces something else good, achievement is good in itself, and it can also be good when its product isn't good but trivial. As long as the process of achieving a goal makes the right kind of change in the world, it has intrinsic worth.

Like items of knowledge, not all achievements have equal value. Equalizing your country's incomes and climbing Everest are major achievements; tying a shoelace or crossing your fingers isn't. There again must be features that explain this difference and make some goals more worth achieving than others. What are they?

GENERALITY: GO BIG!

I think the features that make for better achievements parallel those for better knowledge: the goals most worth achieving are again the most general, in two senses of "general."

The first involves how far a goal extends, or how much of the world it includes. If you cross your fingers, you affect only a couple of fingers on one person's hand. But if you equalize incomes in your whole country, you intentionally change the condition of many people and have a wider impact on the world. Nothing you achieve can extend as far as a scientific law governing the whole universe, but if you affect millions of people rather than just a few, you transfer an idea in your mind to more of reality, or make more of the world match you. This may be one reason why philosophers such as Aristotle have thought the main rival to the philosophical life as the best life possible is not just some life of practical achievement but the political life in particular. Political leaders affect more people and therefore have farther-reaching achievements.

Such achievements are also possible outside politics. A successful businessperson can make it the case that millions of consumers buy her company's product; this too affects many people, albeit in a limited part of their lives. And more modestly extended achievements are possible for a Cub Scout leader who organizes a dozen boys' activities or a hockey coach with a team of twenty; by intentionally affecting more people than just himself he too achieves a broader aim.

Some extended achievements involve cooperation with other people. Imagine that, by tacit or explicit agreement, you cooperate with a dozen neighbors to all put up attractive Halloween displays. If your displays are attractive, then you've all helped to achieve a goal that involves all of you. You yourself may contribute just by working on your own display, but if the others all make theirs attractive, your doing so makes the difference between there being and not being thirteen attractive displays. (Without you there would be just twelve.) And if you intended to help make there be thirteen, then, given what the others did, you intentionally produced a moderately extended result. So extended achievements needn't involve one person's imposing her will on others; they can also result from cooperation among a group of friends.

A goal can also be more extended in time. If you cross your fingers, they normally stay that way for only a few seconds.

But, barring political reversals, a politician who equalizes her country's incomes intends to and does produce an effect that lasts for years. She changes more of the world not only by affecting more people but also by doing so for a longer time. The Roman poet Horace wrote that through his poetry he'd erected a monument "more lasting than bronze," and that's indeed something to be proud of. Willing an effect further into the future is a greater achievement.

This temporal side of extent gives value to any life that's lived according to a long-term plan, or in which large parts have such a plan. At every time in such a life you don't pursue just momentary goals; you also have an aim that involves your life as a whole, lived in a certain way from its early days to its later ones. And if you do end up living that way, and do so because you intended to, then at each time you help make it the case that you live that life, or help achieve a temporally extended end. We can see this as involving a kind of cooperation between your selves at different times, as they work together to achieve a long-term goal involving them all. And their doing so adds worth to what each does.

Of course you can overplan your life: you can think so much about your future that you lose the spontaneity needed for fun, creativity, and love. But then following a life plan isn't the only good in life; it's just one aspect of achievement, which is just one good among others. So if too much planning will deprive you of fun or love, you should forgo it. Even so, successfully following a long-term plan, for all or some of your life, is one thing of worth.

The capacity for extended achievement is again something distinctive of humans. Just as a dog can know only local truths, so it can intend only local goals, such as to eat this bone now.

It can't aim at ends that involve many individuals or extend far into the future; it can't have achievements as good in this respect as ours.

Extended achievement was a central part of Nietzsche's ideal of the powerful or admirable will. He said this will works "on a grander scale in those artists of violence and organizers who build states" and thereby affect not just themselves but "some *other* man, *other* men"; he also said a great individual "can extend his will across great stretches of his life," and looked forward to a "new caste" with "a long, terrible will of its own that would be able to cast its goals millennia hence." Nietzsche's ideal is disturbing when he suggests that the powerful will oppress the weak, forcing them to serve their masters' needs. But if we insist, against him, that there are other goods than achievement, including virtuous concern for others, and that each of us should care as much about others' good as about our own, we can condemn oppression and prefer achievements that benefit rather than harm others. But it will still be one aspect of these achievements' value that they realize goals involving many people and extending through time.

GENERALITY: GO STRUCTURED!

A goal is general in a second sense if, again paralleling knowledge, it has many other goals subordinate to it in a hierarchy. With knowledge the subordination is explanatory: a truth you know is general if you've used it to explain many other truths. With achievement the relation is means-end: a goal is general if you've had to achieve many other goals as means to it, resulting in a structure of achievements like that in Figure 5.1. Here you achieve the two goals in the bottom left as means to the middle one above them, which you achieve along with the other middle one as means to the one on top. The resulting hierarchy again has more value than if you achieved seven unconnected goals. Measuring generality in the same way as we did for knowledge, the achievements in the bottom line have one unit of value each, those in the middle have three each, and the top one has seven, for a total of seventeen units of value in the hierarchy as a whole, which is ten more than in seven unconnected achievements. More complex relationships among mental states, now among achieved goals, again make for greater value.

To contribute value to one of these hierarchies, an item must be an achievement, a goal you pursued intelligently and then realized. (No lucky successes.) And each lower goal must not only help you achieve the ones above it but also

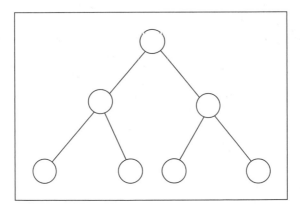

Figure 5.1

have been intended to do so at the time; you must have pursued it at least in part as a means to those higher goals. When all that's so, more means to an end give its achievement more value.

This ideal of means-end generality is again intuitively attractive. If crossing your fingers isn't very valuable, it's partly because it doesn't require many other achievements as means: it's something you do by itself. But changing your country's economy or climbing Everest does require many subordinate means, and the capacity to work through complex series of means is distinctive of humans. Other animals can do one thing in order to achieve a few others, but constructing elaborate hierarchies of goals is something only we do.

The second sense of generality often supports similar recommendations to the first, since more extended goals often require more means to produce. But the two can also diverge. Sometimes a powerful politician can achieve major economic reforms just by raising her hand in a legislative vote; at other times a specific goal, such as your being atop Everest on a specific day, can require many subordinate means.

One place where the second kind of generality reinforces the first is in valuing a life with an overall plan. If you follow such a plan, you not only have a goal that extends beyond the present but also have one with many other goals subordinate to it, involving all the different things you do to fulfill your plan. This plan needn't be very detailed about the future; you can intend just to live a life containing activities X, Y, and Z in some rough proportion. But if you intend everything you do in part as contributing to that life, and you do live it, then each goal you achieve is subordinate to that more general one. Your plan not only extends your interests through time but also unifies them, binding your activities at different times into a coherent whole. The resulting unity is just one good among others and may sometimes have to yield to fun, or love, but just as it's a good to have a goal that extends through your life, so it's a good to have a goal that unifies everything you do.

While few of us unify our whole lives, there's similar value in unifying a part of your life. Even without a plan for all the years you live, you can have one for your teens or forties or just this month. Or you can unify a single aspect of your life. Without having sorted out the relations between your work and personal life, you can have a plan for your career that you pursue through time: maybe to first gain expertise working for a large company and then start a small one of your own. That gives you a hierarchy of goals for one side of your life, even if it's not integrated with the others.

Even when it reinforces extent, means-end generality has distinctive implications. Just as there's more hierarchical value in knowledge that explains a wide variety of truths, so the best achievements require a variety of means. Imagine that, like Charlie Chaplin in *Modern Times*, you work on an old-fashioned assembly line. You may intend many individual acts as means to earning your day's pay but, intuitively, your labor has little value. That's because your acts are all of the same type—all pullings of this lever or pushings of that knob. So though you achieve many individual ends in your day's hierarchy, you don't achieve many *kinds* of end or much means-end generality. Now imagine that you're establishing a new business. Here your workday, aimed ultimately at making your business a success, can include decisions about product design, manufacturing, hiring, marketing, and more. That's a much greater variety of subordinate goals and makes for a more valuable achievement.

But then the best life plans will also involve variety. The British writer Leonard Woolf (husband of Virginia) did many different things in his life: he was a civil servant in colonial Ceylon for ten years, then a book publisher, magazine editor, political activist, and more. His sequence of careers wasn't planned in advance, but imagine that it was, so he intended from the start to change his line of work every ten years. His life plan would then have more value, because of its variety, than if he intended to and did work all his life in Ceylon. He would still have an extended and unifying goal, though now to lead a life of frequent change, but the activities this goal demanded would be more diverse.

GENERALITY: GO COMPLEX!

These initial implications of means-end generality concern the overall structure of your life, but others concern your choice of particular activities.

Think of some activities that seem valuable, such as chess, mountain climbing, and running a political campaign. If we ask what makes them good, the answer is surely in part that they're difficult, requiring skill and concentration. This even seems part of the meaning of the word "achievement": we don't call crossing your fingers an achievement because it's too easy. Achievements have to be challenging, and the more challenging the better.

But what makes an activity difficult is largely its means-end complexity. You have a goal such as checkmating your opponent or standing atop Everest, but to achieve it you have to achieve many other goals as means to it. You move a pawn to maintain your defensive position, so you can safely make a certain attack later, which will capture a rook and lead to checkmate. Getting to the top of a mountain requires many preparatory acts of training, equipment selection, and more, followed by all the different moves you make during your climb. These activities involve on a smaller scale the same structuring of goals found in a unified life, with many lower down in a hierarchy serving one above.

As in a unified life, this structuring has more value the more varied its component parts. There's some variety in chess, given the game's different pieces and its offensive and defensive sides, but there's more in mountain climbing or political campaigning. In the last of these you have to coordinate policy development, advertising, fund-raising, polling, and more to reach your electoral goal, which adds to the activity's value.

Means-end generality makes for difficulty in several ways. First, the more subordinate goals an activity involves, the more places there are where it can go wrong and failure can prevent you from achieving your final goal. If an activity requires just two subordinate achievements, there are two ways it can fail; if it requires a hundred, there are many more. In addition, the more complex the arrangement of these goals, the more skill it takes to monitor your progress through them and achieve them in the right sequence. Doing that with two subordinate goals requires a little executive skill; doing it with a hundred requires much more. And an activity's difficulty is heightened if its hierarchy contains goals of different kinds. Then you don't need just one skill to complete it; you need many, as well as greater executive skill to coordinate them.

Activities are also harder the more precision they require. We saw how with more precise knowledge you both know and can explain more truths, and something similar holds for achievement. If I hit an approach shot in golf, what I can intend with a justified belief that I'll succeed is only to put the ball somewhere near the green. My shot will always finish in a precise spot, occasionally close to the hole. But when that happens, the result isn't something I intended in the relevant way and therefore achieved—it was only luck. By contrast, Tiger Woods can intend to put his ball not only on the green but to the left of the hole, from where he has an uphill putt, and within ten feet. He can intend and therefore achieve more precise goals than I, which gives him more items in his hierarchy of golfing goals and, especially, more items subordinate to his main one of shooting a low score.

And the best activities demand precision. A skilled poet chooses not just some word to complete a line but the specific one that best fits his meter, rhyme, and meaning. A chess master moves his queen only when an opening exists, a carpenter cuts the exact length of wood he needs, and a skilled drummer delays his backbeat not just somewhat but a precise amount. The precision of these activities increases their difficulty, since it's harder to achieve more exact goals, and also increases their value. If we admire poets, carpenters, and drummers, it's partly for achieving such finely crafted results.

Difficult activities also often involve a kind of extent. If I look at a chessboard, I see just some individual pieces with individual relationships between them but no overall pattern. But that pattern is just what a chess master does see:

he takes in the collection of pieces as a single pattern of forces, strengths, and weaknesses, and when he moves a piece it's mainly to give that pattern one overall shape rather than another. What I see only as isolated bits, his mind comprehends as a single whole. The same happens in sports: Wayne Gretzky and Michael Jordan could see the hockey or basketball play around them as a unified whole, know where their teammates and opponents would be next, and act on that knowledge. Or consider hearing a melody for the first time. Many of us will hear the individual notes and transitions between them but not yet grasp the melody as a whole; that's why we can't sing it back. But a trained musician can sing it back, because he already hears it as a unit, its various tones forming a single pattern. Likewise in visual art. Here's how Henry Moore was said to view one of his sculptures:

> He thinks of it, whatever its size, as if he were holding it completely enclosed in the hollow of his hand: he mentally visualizes a complex form *from all round itself*; he knows while he looks at one side what the other side is like; he identifies himself with its centre of gravity, its mass, its weight; he realizes its volume, as the space that the shape displaces in the air.

He too could stretch his mind around an extended state of affairs, now a three-dimensional sculpture, and manipulate it in light of its global properties. In all these fields the best achieve not only hierarchically structured goals but also extended ones.

The need for such goals again increases an activity's difficulty. Grasping chess positions, melodies, or sculptures as wholes is hard, and something only a few people can do. Even those with innate talent for it need years of repeated chess games, musical exercises, or sculptings to get to where they can do it at will.

The value of difficult activities is combined with that of knowledge in the search for knowledge or for new discoveries, which some have valued above knowledge itself. The eighteenth-century playwright Gotthold Lessing wrote that if God offered him the choice between truth and the search for truth, he would unhesitatingly choose the search for truth. The philosopher Nicolas Malebranche said that if he held truth captive in his hand, he would open his hand and let it fly, so he could again pursue and capture it. But a successful search for knowledge is really an instance of achievement. A researcher sets herself a goal—discovering a grand unified theory or the causes of World War I—and uses skill and ingenuity to achieve it. She works through a hierarchy of means, involving individual experiments or bits of research, until she achieves her final aim. While it's impressive that physicists know facts going back to the big bang and out to the edges of the universe, it's also impressive that they arrived at that knowledge in the way they did, by extracting it from nature's limited clues. Though their research resulted in knowledge, it was also a tremendous achievement.

As with knowledge, the value in difficult activities isn't just open to an elite. While most of us can't play grandmaster-level chess or sculpt like Henry Moore, our engaging in activities like these at a more modest level can embody similar values. We can pursue moderately complex chess strategies and achieve somewhat precise goals, and the same is true in everyday pursuits such as gardening and raising children.

There too we can intend some goals as means to others and work through them in sequence. The value of means-end generality doesn't have a sharp cutoff; there's a continuous scale from lower to higher, and any point on that scale has some worth.

Though the features that make particular activities good mirror those found in a unified life, realizing these features at the two levels can conflict. If you lead the most organized life you can, your particular activities may not be as good as they could be, whereas making those activities best can require living more from day to day. Consider an artist who often changed his creative style, such as Picasso or Bob Dylan. Maybe to produce his best work he needed not to have a life plan but always to have some new style to throw himself into. The result may have been a less coherent artistic career than one that keeps refining the same style—like Poussin's or B. B. King's—but also one with better individual works than if Picasso or Dylan had aimed at a unified career. By contrast, Poussin or B. B. King might have produced worse works if they'd tried changing styles. The same elements make for achievement in your whole life and in particular activities, but while the two sometimes reinforce each other, they can also pull in different directions.

PLAYING GAMES

The value of achievement hasn't been much recognized by philosophers, in part because it can be hard to see. In achievement you realize a goal, but often that goal is good in itself: more equal incomes in your society or happiness for a friend.

But then the process of achieving the goal is good as a means, or for what it produces, and that can be the most important thing about it. Imagine that a hundred years ago a settler on the Canadian prairie successfully plows his land, builds a house, and harvests his first crop. Given its difficulty, his achievement is good in itself, but it also gives his family food and shelter for the winter and the prospect of a secure life in the future. The importance of these results can overshadow the intrinsic value of his work and make the latter harder to see.

The value of achievement is therefore most clearly visible when its product isn't good but trivial—as it is paradigmatically in games.

Excellence in games is certainly something we value. In Canada hockey players are named to the highest level of the Order of Canada, while in Britain footballers and cricketers are made MBE and even knighted; we likewise admire chess champions and those who excel at games such as Scrabble. Whatever our other ideals, we think excellence in a sport or game is worth pursuing. Even if you play just on weekends, being good at a game is good.

But what exactly are games, and what do they have in common that makes them games? An illuminating answer from the philosopher Bernard Suits also explains why skill in games is the purest expression of the value of achievement.

Despite their many differences, Suits says, all games share three features. First, in playing a game you pursue a goal that can be understood and achieved apart from the game. In golf this is that a ball go into a hole in the ground, in mountain climbing that you stand atop a mountain, in the 200-meter sprint that you cross a line on the track before your competitors. Second, the game has rules, and these rules forbid you to take the most efficient means to your goal. In golf you can't pick the ball up, walk down the fairway, and drop it in the hole by hand; you have to advance it using clubs, play it where it lies, and so on. In mountain climbing you can't take a helicopter to the summit; in the 200 meters you can't cut across the infield or start before your competitors. Finally, if you're to count as playing a game, you need a certain attitude. Return to the settler who establishes a farm on the prairie. If he uses only his own muscles, he may wish he had oxen to help him or, looking forward in time, a combine harvester. If he doesn't have these, he pursues his goal by less than the most efficient means, but he isn't playing a game. For that he'd have to willingly accept the limits the rules impose, or do so because he wants to engage in the activity of pursuing his goal using only the methods they allow. A golfer doesn't wish he could drop his ball in the hole by hand; he wants to play golf, which doesn't allow that. A climber doesn't want to fly to the peak, and a sprinter doesn't want to take a shortcut; they too want to stick to the rules. So the final defining feature of a game is that you accept the restrictions the rules impose because you want to play the game.

The third of these features, about your attitude, can make game playing virtuous, but the first two make it an occasion for achievement. They give you a goal and then make achieving it not only more difficult than it could be but also, at least in games worth excelling at, by absolute standards reasonably difficult. (Rock, paper, scissors isn't difficult, but it's not a game worth excelling at.) They can't make achieving the goal impossible; then no one would play the game. But for a game to be worth investing time in, it has to be a challenge. Then succeeding at it—checkmating your opponent or scaling the mountain—involves doing something with many of the elements of difficulty we've discussed, such as a complex hierarchy of means and varied, extended ends.

But now the activity can be good *only* intrinsically and not as a means. That's because a game's initial goal is almost always trivial: there's no value in itself in a ball's going in a hole in the ground or your standing atop a mountain. In playing a good game you pursue a valueless end but go through a complex and difficult process to achieve it, and the value of your doing so can reside only in the process considered apart from its result. For your activity to have its full value, you have to achieve your end: you have to get the ball in the hole or reach the mountain peak. But your activity's value doesn't depend on any value its end has in itself, being instead entirely one of process rather than product, journey rather than destination. When you play a game, you pursue a goal and don't fully succeed unless you achieve that goal, but the value of your achievement is independent of that goal's goodness considered on its own.

This makes achievement what I'll call a paradigmatically modern, as against classical, value. Aristotle expressed the classical view when he said that if an activity has a goal outside itself, it can't have more value than that goal does. On this basis he dismissed the life of moneymaking as worthless: since having money has no value in itself, the activity of getting it must likewise have no value. But what I'm calling a modern view says that pursuing a goal can have value just in itself, because it's difficult or demands precision. Marx thought that in his utopia people would have material production, or making things, as their "prime want." Now, you can't produce unless you produce some thing: your activity has to aim at some separate result like a finished table or constructed house. But in Marx's utopia these end results wouldn't be needed in themselves, since people would already live in plenty. They'd therefore produce for producing's sake, or just to engage in the process of making. Similarly, Nietzsche wanted people to have both extended goals and ones that unify their lives; the second was another part of his ideal of a powerful will. But he didn't care what this goal was, so long as it was extended and unifying—you could organize your life around anything. He too valued the process of transferring an idea to reality without regard to its value in itself; he too had the modern view that values process independently of product.

Though best illustrated by games, this modern value is also found elsewhere. Consider business activity. It also aims at a goal and isn't successful unless it achieves that goal. But often this goal is intrinsically trivial: the world's no better if people drink Coke rather than Pepsi or use Blu-Ray rather than HD DVDs. But the process of achieving a business goal can be extremely difficult, requiring a CEO and her employees to make many subtle, precise, and interrelated decisions. When these decisions succeed and the company comes to dominate its market, the people who achieved that are widely admired. There are business as well as sports halls of fame; Bill Gates and Warren Buffett are not only envied for their wealth but also, and as much, admired for the skill by which they acquired it. A life in business is often devoted to pursuing a goal with little worth in itself, but it can have significant value if the process of reaching that goal calls on enough sophisticated skills—in other words, if business is a good enough game.

MAKE YOURSELF

Another aspect of a good life is that you make it yourself: you determine its contents and contours rather than having them forced upon you. You choose where you'll live, whom you'll marry, and what work you'll do. You're self-determining—which is another kind of achievement.

Consider two people who farm. One does so because it was his only life option other than starving or begging. The other could have chosen many careers: he could have been a forester, computer programmer, newspaper writer, and more, but preferred farming. Even if the two farm in similar ways, isn't the second person's life better? He got to choose his career from an array of alternatives rather than being forced into it; he made his own life rather than having it made for him.

Of course the first farmer did decide to farm rather than starve or beg, so if we ask why he's a farmer, the answer is that he chose it. But if we ask why he's not a forester or pro-grammer, the answer turns not on any choice of his but on whatever external factors made those careers unavailable to him. If we ask why the second farmer isn't a forester or pro-grammer, however, the answer does turn on his choice. He made it the case that he isn't in one of those careers by deciding not to be.

He therefore determined more facts about his life than the first farmer. He willed not only to be a farmer but also not to be a forester, programmer, or writer, and he realized all those goals, the negative as well as the positive. He therefore achieved more goals within his life, and also had more goals in a hierarchy topped by farming; his greater self-determination involved greater achievement.

The main precondition for this achievement is freedom. You have to have and know you have many life options, so you can exercise choice among them; you need a wider rather than narrower range of choice. Freedom obviously has instrumental value, since with more options you may have better options. (The first farmer might have had a better life if he'd been able to choose forestry.) But it's also needed for the intrinsic good of self-determination.

This good requires as well that you choose in the fullest sense among your options: you have to consider both farming and forestry and then prefer the first rather than be driven to it by some psychological compulsion. Choosing not to do things probably isn't as valuable as choosing to do them; your life isn't significantly better if you know all the flavors of ice cream at a Baskin-Robbins and consciously reject the others when you order chocolate. But choosing against large life options—against decades of forestry or programming—does seem to have worth, or at least the self-determination it involves has worth. And it may even have special worth. We saw that knowing your relation to your surroundings has extra value just because of its subject matter; maybe achievements in your life, of the kind that make for self-determination, also have extra value because they're about you.

If you chart your own life course, you decide both what your life will contain and what it won't. You're autonomous rather than the plaything of circumstance, and that's a final instance of the value of achievement.

FURTHER READINGS

Philosophers haven't discussed the value of achievement much, often taking the only good on the active side of our nature to be specifically moral virtue. Nietzsche's comments about extended willing come in *On the Genealogy of Morals*, *The Will to Power*, and *Beyond Good and Evil*; his remark connecting a powerful will to a unified will is in *The Will to Power*. I discuss generality as a measure of the value of achievements, and develop the parallel with knowledge, in chaps. 8–10 of my *Perfectionism*. Bernard Suits's analysis of games is given in *The Grasshopper: Games, Life, and Utopia*. This wonderfully written book, a loving parody of a Platonic dialogue with the Grasshopper from Aesop's fable in the role of Socrates, also argues that game playing is the supreme human good, because in utopia it would be everyone's main activity.

Chapter Six

BEING GOOD

They smiled at the good / And frowned at the bad.

—Ludwig Bemelmans, *Madeline*

We've added knowledge and achievement to the list of goods because hedonism can find high value in a life of mindless pleasure, but hedonism also values vicious pleasures such as sadistic pleasure in another's pain. It says that, their effects aside, these pleasures are purely good and compassionate pain at another's pain is bad. If someone is hurting, it only makes things worse if you hurt with him; far better if his pain gives you a kick.

But surely this is backward: it's compassion that's good and sadism that's bad. And this is true not only of individual feelings but also of your whole life. To live a good life you need to be happy, understand things, and achieve worthwhile goals. But shouldn't you also be a good person? If you devote yourself to deliberately hurting others, won't that make your life worse?

We should therefore add moral virtue to the list of goods and vice to the evils, and many philosophers have done this. In fact, some have thought virtue the greatest of all human goods, so the value of your life depends primarily on how virtuous you are. I'll argue against this last claim, but I certainly agree that virtue is one intrinsic good, or one part of a valuable life. The world is better if people care about each other than if they're malicious, and your own life will be better if, though somewhat less happy, it's more benevolent and less self-involved.

What exactly is virtue? We can list individual virtues such as compassion, courage, and modesty, but what do they have in common that makes them virtues? An illuminating answer will also explain why virtue is valuable, or why being a good person is good.

LOVING GOODS AND HATING EVILS

Consider our original examples of sadistic or malicious pleasure and compassionate pain. Each involves an attitude, in particular a pleasure or pain that something is the case, but other attitudes too can be virtuous or vicious. If it's malicious to be pleased by another's pain, it's likewise malicious to want her pain for its own sake or try to inflict it on her; these too are forms of malice. And it's compassionate to hope her pain ends and try to make that happen. As well as pleasures and pains, desires and intentions can also embody virtue and vice.

In fact, virtue and vice always involve an attitude, and the attitude's object is something with a positive or negative moral quality. In our examples it's another person's pain, which is an evil, but there are also virtues and vices directed at goods. If you want another's pleasure for its own sake, try to promote his pleasure, and are pleased when he feels it, then you're benevolent. But if you're pained by his pleasure—if you wish he weren't feeling it and try to destroy it—you show a malicious form of envy.

And what separates the virtues from the vices is that the former involve a morally fitting attitude toward their object while the latter involve an unfitting one. Thus, benevolence is a virtue because it involves a positive attitude toward the good of another's pleasure; its positive orientation—its being *for* the pleasure—matches its object's positive value. Likewise, compassion involves a negative attitude toward pain, or being against a negative value, and it's virtuous for that reason. (Virtue is therefore like boosting one car battery from another: you want to connect positive to positive and negative to negative.) But the opposite attitudes are unfitting and therefore morally vicious. Malicious pleasure involves a positive attitude toward a negative value and envy a negative attitude toward a positive one, neither of which matches its object's value. Another person's pleasure is good, for example, but your envious desire to destroy it is aimed against it.

If that's what virtue is, though, we can explain why virtue's good if we accept the general principle that it's intrinsically good to have fitting attitudes toward values and evil to have unfitting ones, or good to love goods and hate evils and evil to do the opposite. If another person's pleasure is good, having a positive attitude toward it is another good thing; if her pain is evil, being pleased by it is another evil. Being for goods is good and being against them is evil, so what makes an attitude virtuous or vicious at the same time makes it good or evil.

This general principle is attractive: it seems intuitively right that loving the good is good and hating it is evil. The principle also has a philosophical history. Aristotle said that if an activity is good, pleasure in it is also good, whereas if an activity is bad, pleasure in it is bad. And that's just a specific application of a principle later philosophers such as Moore would state in a more general form.

Taken together, these ideas make virtue a higher-level good, one that involves a certain relation to other intrinsic goods and evils. Its being so means that virtue can't be the only intrinsic good. There have to be other values it responds properly to, and these needn't be just pleasure and pain. If knowledge is intrinsically good, then desiring and pursuing knowledge because you just want to understand is also virtuous and good; it involves a fitting attitude toward knowledge. (This is another merit of the search for knowledge: as well as involving achievement when it's successful, it can reflect an intense love of knowledge.) Conversely, if false belief, the opposite of knowledge, is evil, then wanting or being pleased by another's errors is evil. Similarly for achievement: seeking excellence in chess or music for its own sake is virtuous, while hating another's excellence is evil.

The objects of virtue can even be states that stretch across individuals. Some people think certain distributions of pleasure across people are intrinsically good and, more specifically, just—maybe equal distributions or ones proportioned to people's deserts. If so, loving these distributions for themselves—say, wanting equal distributions and being pleased by them—involves a distinctive virtue of justice and hating them is unjust. But the basic idea remains that attitudes of loving good and hating evil are virtuous and good, and their contraries vicious and evil.

This idea can be applied back on its own results. If loving anything good is good, then that loving is another thing it's good to love. Let's say Bob enjoys an innocent pleasure, and Carol's benevolently pleased by his pleasure: she's happy that he's happy. Her benevolence is virtuous and good, which means that if someone else loves it for itself, that too is good. So if Ted's pleased that Carol's pleased by Bob's pleasure, Ted's pleasure is another good love of a good. And the same is true if Alice's pleased that Ted's pleased that Carol's pleased by Bob's pleasure. The more complex these attitudes become, the less common they are and, in my view, the less value they have. If the chain of pleasure in another's pleasure in another's pleasure gets very long, the resulting value becomes very small. But in principle the idea can be repeated to infinity, since any time an attitude is good or evil, it's something there's further value in loving or hating for itself.

And in some cases this further value is important. Let's say you're not now compassionate but want to be, and take steps to try to become so. You go to shelters for the homeless, hoping that seeing others' troubles close up will make you care about them more. Or you read novels about compassionate people, hoping to be inspired. In wanting to become compassionate you're wanting something good, and while not as good as compassion itself, that's still good to some degree. When the young Queen Victoria said "I will be good," she showed that to some extent she already was.

Or imagine that you have envious thoughts about a friend—you wish he weren't quite so successful—and feel shame about that fact. Your shame is a negative emotion toward something evil, and therefore good: it hates a love of evil, which is virtuous. There can also be vices of this kind. Think of a Hollywood villain such as the Joker in *Batman*, as played by Jack Nicholson. He's malicious, wanting to hurt other people and cause them pain. But he also takes pleasure in his malice, cackling gleefully as he hatches his wicked plans; he delights in his vice and the hurtful feelings toward others it involves. He also delights in the vice of his underlings—he cackles at how they too want to hurt others—and hates Batman's and Robin's virtue. If virtue is good and vice evil, we should love the former and hate the latter. By doing the opposite the Joker compounds the evil of his malice with the higher-level evils of loving malice and hating benevolence.

In all these virtues the object is a good or an evil, but there's another possibility. If you think an act is right and perform it because it's right, you act conscientiously, or from a sense of duty, and that too is virtuous. Just as it's good to love what's good, so it's virtuous and good to care about what's morally required and try to do it. You again have a positive attitude toward a positive moral quality, though now toward an act's rightness rather than the goodness of a state of affairs. But the attitude's still fitting: an act's being right is something positive about it and makes your being for it appropriate. So there's another attitude that's virtuous: wanting to do what's right because it's right. And wanting to do wrong because it's wrong, if that's psychologically possible, is a horrible form of vice.

TWO FACES OF VIRTUE

Conscientiousness involves a moral judgment: to do an act because it's right, you must first be thinking of it as right. And you can likewise want something good because it's good, or because you think it has value. You have the evaluative thought that, say, scientific knowledge is good, and pursue it because you want what's good. Some philosophers have believed that action guided by evaluative thoughts is the most or even only virtuous action. Kant, for example, thought that only acts motivated by a sense of duty have moral worth; any others, no matter how compassionate or caring, are valueless.

But surely that's wrong. While you can pursue scientific knowledge because you think it's good, you can also do so from simple curiosity; without any evaluative thoughts, you just want to understand. Then you want something good—knowledge—for the very property that makes it good: that it's knowledge. And that still seems virtuous. You have a positive attitude toward a good based on a quality that makes it good, which orients you positively to something positive.

Or imagine that you want me to be happy. You can believe my happiness is good and want it for that reason, or without thinking about goodness you can just want me to feel good. Here your desire for my happiness doesn't depend on an evaluative belief but is immediate. Isn't that still virtuous? The Scottish philosopher David Hume thought we're all born with natural tendencies to be pleased by others' pleasures and pained by their pains. If he were right, we'd all be born naturally virtuous.

Likewise for attitudes toward right acts, much as Kant would protest. In a situation where you'd benefit from telling a lie, you can decide not to because you think lying's wrong. But you can also just naturally dislike lying, or without thoughts about wrongness find it repellent, and that too is a form of virtue. You avoid a wrong act for the feature that makes it wrong, which is fitting and therefore good.

Let's call attitudes based on evaluative thoughts "moralized" and ones not so based "simply emotional." Then there are both moralized and simply emotional forms of virtue, and an ideal person will have both. He'll want scientific knowledge both because he thinks it's good and from natural curiosity, and he'll avoid lying both because he thinks it's wrong and because he just dislikes it. Plato and Aristotle thought virtue involves a harmony between the rational and non-rational parts of your soul, so that both want the same thing. If you're temperate, you know which foods are healthy and want to eat them because they're healthy (your rational part), but you also have no appetite for unhealthy foods (your non-rational part). You wouldn't enjoy an extra dessert if you had one, but you do love your lentils.

That's also the idea here. One part of our psyche makes judgments about what's good and right and generates motives from them, while another has simple desires not based on evaluative thoughts. And there's harmony within us when our simple desires are for the same things our judgments say are good or right.

While Kant thought only moralized attitudes have value, a less radical view says only that these attitudes are better, so it's best to be motivated mostly by evaluative thoughts. This sometimes seems right. A judge who treats prosecution and defense equally because that's her duty seems more admirable than one who just likes being even-handed; likewise for a scientist who pursues knowledge because he thinks it's good rather than just from curiosity.

But at other times the opposite seems true. Imagine that you're in the hospital recovering from a painful operation and a friend comes at considerable inconvenience to visit you. When you say how much you appreciate her visit and the concern for you it shows, she says it isn't that she cares for you; she just knew that as a friend, she had a duty to visit. You insist that she must care, but as your conversation progresses you realize that she's telling the truth and her main motive for visiting was just to do her duty.

Don't you now think less of her as a friend and even as a person? A real friend would care about you directly, from simple emotion rather than just because of a belief about duty. She might also have that belief and be partly motivated by it; it might even be better if she was. But her main impulse for visiting, or for doing anything with you, would be simple love, or a simple desire for your company and happiness. The best friends, unlike the best judges or scientists, are moved more by simple feeling than by evaluative judgment.

So the ideal mix of moralized and simple virtue may differ in different contexts. But both are forms of virtue, and both are part of an ideally good life. A fully virtuous person wants what's good and right both because it's good or right and because, evaluative thoughts aside, he simply does.

THE VARIETY OF VICES

Tolstoy famously said that all happy families are alike but every unhappy family is unhappy in its own way. Aristotle said something similar: that while there's only one way to be vir-tuous, there are many ways to be vicious. And there are indeed several.

The vices we've discussed so far—call them simple vices—involve wrongly oriented attitudes, such as malicious pleasure in another's pain or envy of his joy. But imagine that a tor-turer, while not positively enjoying his victim's pain, just isn't bothered by it. He doesn't care about the suffering he causes and feels no compunction about inflicting it: he's totally indif-ferent. We could say his not caring puts him in a neutral state between virtue and vice, but that doesn't seem right. His indifference to another's pain is callous, and callousness is a vice rather than just the absence of a virtue: it's positively evil rather than just not good. The same is true if someone is indifferent about a great good he could produce: he could develop an artistic talent or bring others great joy, but he can't be bothered. That's sloth or apathy, and those too are vices rather than just the lack of a virtue.

So it's not only wrongly oriented attitudes that are vicious; so is not having right ones, or not caring where a good person would care. And even rightly oriented attitudes can be vicious if they're insufficiently strong. Imagine that a torturer cares only a tiny bit about his victim's pain, or a soldier liberating a concentration camp at the end of World War II is just slightly saddened by what he sees, as he might be by a friend's head-ache. These attitudes are so inadequate to their objects' evil that they too involve callousness. Great values demand strong responses, and ones that fall too far short are evil.

These vices of indifference, as I'll call them, aren't as evil as the simple vices: being callous about another's pain isn't as bad as taking sadistic pleasure in it. But they're still vices, and like the simple ones can have an object that's itself a virtue or vice. Imagine that the Joker in *Batman* doesn't delight in his malicious desires but also isn't disturbed by them. He doesn't feel the shame at his malice that a (partly) good person would feel; that he wants others to suffer doesn't bother him a bit. He's then shameless about his malice, and shamelessness is again not just the lack of a virtue but a vice, one of being indifferent to evil. And it's likewise a vice to be only slightly ashamed of a serious vice, for example, only mildly troubled by your extreme sadism.

There's a third kind of vice. If you're ideally virtuous, you'll not only love goods and hate evils but do so in proportion to their degrees of value, caring as much more about greater goods or evils as they're greater. If one person feels much more pain than another, you'll be much more saddened by the former's pain; if you can give a little pleasure to one person or a lot to another, you'll want to do the second a lot more. If there are many goods and evils, you'll divide your concern among them in a way that matches their degrees of value.

None of us reaches this ideal completely, and small departures from it involve only a shortfall in virtue rather than any positive vice. If you want a four-times-as-great pleasure only three times as much, your attitudes may still be on balance good—not quite as good as they could be but not positively bad. But larger disproportions, where you want a much smaller good a great deal more, *are* positively bad: dividing your concerns that disproportionately is evil. This yields a final family of vices of disproportion.

One of these is selfishness, where you care much more about your own minor pleasures than about other people's larger pleasures or very great pains. Since your own pleasure is good, your wanting it is also good, and your wanting it more can even in itself always be better. But if you care much more about your own pleasure than about other people's, your attitudes are out of proportion, and by enough to make them, taken together, vicious. Extreme selfishness is not just less than ideally good but bad.

Likewise for extreme cowardice. A coward cares more about avoiding hurt or danger for himself than about some greater good he could achieve by risking that hurt. Maybe he could save another person's life or help defend his country, but he's too afraid to and so does nothing. He cares more about the lesser good of avoiding his own pain than about something much more important—which is again disproportionate enough to be evil.

So there are three kinds of vice. First are the simple vices, involving a wrongly oriented attitude such as loving an evil or hating a good; they're typified by malice and envy. Next come the vices of indifference, where without having a wrongly oriented attitude you lack a right one; these include callousness and sloth. Last come the vices of disproportion, where your attitudes are appropriately oriented and maybe on their own good, but so out of proportion to their objects' values that taken together they're evil; here we find selfishness and cowardice. And there are further vices in each category.

Consider cynicism. It's an ugly trait, one you wouldn't want your child to grow up with. But why? A cynic thinks the world's a bad place. He thinks most people are at bottom selfish, their apparent concern for others only a show, while the few genuinely unselfish souls are exploited, so only the bastards thrive. So far the cynic is being pessimistic, and mere pessimism isn't a vice. While a pessimist's false beliefs about the world (assuming they are false) make him gloomier than he need be, he can still have virtuous attitudes: he can be saddened by the evil he thinks he sees and wish people and their lives were better.

That's where a cynic differs. Far from being saddened by people's selfishness, he secretly delights in it; he wants the world to be bad and by wishful thinking persuades himself that it is. (Maybe he sees evil in himself and can't stand the thought that others are better.) The dictionary defines a cynic as one who "doubts or despises human sincerity or merit," but it's the despising that's central and that explains the doubting. A cynic denies human goodness because he hates it and wants it not to exist, and that makes his cynicism a simple vice.

Now consider thoughtlessness, where you hurt someone because you weren't thinking about what you were doing, or break a promise because you forgot you made it. These cases don't involve indifference of the brazen kind found in callousness and sloth, where you know an act has bad features but do it anyway. But they still involve indifference, because they involve not bothering to know. If you really want not to hurt others, you'll carefully watch out for things that will; you'll know which acts may wound people and avoid them for that reason. And if you care about keeping promises, you'll be sure to remember any you make. So thoughtlessness is another vice of indifference: of not caring enough to know things you ought to know.

Finally, consider pride. For Christians this is the worst vice of all—it brought Satan down—and in humans it involves a massively false belief. When you're proud you think your character or something you've done is comparatively good, but according to Christianity that's never the case. After the Fall we're all wretches, infinitely beneath God's goodness, and should feel only shame and guilt about ourselves. But if there's no God, then some of us really are comparatively good. What's wrong with knowing that and feeling proud of it?

In principle there's nothing wrong, but the danger is in excessive pride, or being more pleased by a trait or achievement than its value, especially compared to other people's, makes appropriate. You're not just somewhat pleased by what you've done but dwell on it, revel in it, and want to boast of it to other people. You care much more about it than about similar achievements by others, and that's a vice of disproportion. Excessive pride often goes with exaggerating your merits: you take disproportionate pleasure in what you've done because you think it's better than it is. But you do that because you want to be better than other people and convince yourself by wishful thinking that you are. I've said that exaggerating your talents can stimulate you to develop them more, and it can. But when its origin is a selfish desire to be better than other people, it also involves a nasty vice of pride. That's why for some of us the only antidote to pride is an almost excessive modesty: not thinking of our merits and even underestimating them, so we can avoid the more common vice of being too taken with them.

Of the three kinds of vice, the simple ones are in the abstract the worst, followed by those of indifference and then of disproportion. It's worse to take pleasure in another's pain than not to care about it, and worse not to care than to care less about it than about your own pain. But this abstract ranking doesn't extend to all particular cases. If I go out of my way to cause you a minor pain, my petty malice is vicious but not very vicious. If I'm indifferent to your intense pain, however, that's very vicious. Hannah Arendt's concept of "the banality of evil," applied initially to Adolf Eichmann, is precisely that of someone who causes enormous evil not from sadism or malice but with bland indifference, and indifference to an evil as enormous as the Holocaust is far worse than petty malice. Similarly, caring less about the Holocaust than about some minor good such as advancement in your career, which Eichmann did as well, is also worse than petty malice. How bad a vice is depends both on the kind of attitude it involves and on its object, so a less unfitting attitude toward a greater good or evil can be a greater moral vice. While malice is in general worse than selfishness, petty malice can be less evil than gross self-absorption.

Though there are the three kinds of vice, there's really just one form of virtue (remember Tolstoy on happy families): having rightly oriented attitudes that are at least roughly proportioned to their objects' values. A benevolent desire for others' pleasure, fairly close in intensity to your desire for your own pleasure; a yearning for knowledge, in rough proportion to its importance; shame at any malice or envy you feel; and a courageous willingness to sacrifice your comfort for greater goods, especially for other people: these are all different instances of the one basic form of virtue.

THE GREATEST GOOD?

If virtue is good, then even apart from any effects on you or others, your life is better if you're benevolent and courageous rather than malicious or cowardly. But *how* good is virtue? How does its value compare with other goods such as pleasure and achievement?

Some philosophers have thought virtue immensely important. In the *Republic*, Plato has Socrates argue that it's better to be a just person who's scorned and despised than to have riches, power, and friends but be unjust—the virtue, he insists, matters more. The Stoics thought a virtuous life best no matter what else it involves, and in the nineteenth century John Henry Newman said it would be better if the whole human race died "in extremest agony" than if one person committed one venial sin.

These are high-minded views, in fact too high-minded to be credible. Aristotle was surely being sensible when he rejected as ludicrous the idea that you can lead a good life while being tortured. And far from being the greatest good, virtue is in my view a lesser good in the following sense: if virtue involves caring appropriately about some other good or bad thing, it always has less value than that thing. When it involves loving some good, it's less good than that good, and it's also less good than an evil it hates is evil. Let's consider some examples.

If you feel compassion for a friend's pain, your compassion is good and makes the overall situation better than if you didn't care about her pain. But it can't be more good than her pain is evil. It can't be better for there to be pain and compassion for that pain than for there to be no pain and no compassion; the compassion must be the lesser value. Likewise for shame. If you have a malicious desire and feel ashamed of it, that's better than if you felt no shame about your malice. But your shame can't be more good than the malice is evil: it can't be better to want to hurt others and feel bad about it than not to want to hurt them.

These points bear on the well-known "argument from evil" against the existence of God. If God is all-powerful and perfectly good, the argument asks, how could he have created a world with all the pain we see around us? Doesn't its existence disprove his? To this some theists respond that pain is necessary for there to be higher goods such as compassion and bravery, and that's why God created it. But the problem is that these *aren't* higher goods: compassion is less good than the pain it cares about is evil, so a God who created pain in order to allow compassion would be creating more evil than good.

A similar point applies to loves of the good. Imagine that a teacher teaches her students from a benevolent desire that they gain knowledge, and they do gain knowledge. What should you as an observer be more pleased by: that she taught from a virtuous motive or that her students learned? Surely you should be more pleased that the students learned—but then that must have more value. Or imagine that an uncaring teacher is teaching using ineffective methods, so his students aren't learning, and you can either change his attitude while leaving his methods unchanged or improve his methods but not his attitude. Surely you should change his methods, which again implies that his attitude matters less.

The same holds for vicious attitudes. If a torturer is causing a victim intense pain while taking sadistic pleasure in that pain, you should be more saddened by the pain than by the sadism. And if you can either stop the torturer's pleasure while leaving his machine running or secretly disconnect his machine, you should disconnect the machine. But then again his sadism must be less bad. Those who think vice the greatest evil, such as the Stoics and Newman, are committed to leaving the machine running if that will let them improve the sadist's character—which is surely appalling.

That virtue is a lesser good also explains why very complex attitudes such as Ted's pleasure in Carol's pleasure in Bob's pleasure have such little value. If the value of an attitude is always less than that of its object, the value of iterated loves of the good gets progressively smaller: Carol's pleasure is less good than Bob's, Ted's is less good than Carol's, and so on.

So there are several reasons why virtue and vice have less value than their objects, but it doesn't follow that they always have less value than other instances of pleasure, pain, or knowledge. If I feel compassion for your intense pain, my compassion is less good than your pain is evil, but it can have more value than a minor pleasure of mine, like that of eating a chocolate. Your pain is much more evil than the pleasure of the chocolate is good, and the value of my compassion can therefore fall between the two: less than the evil of the pain but more than the goodness of the pleasure. Or consider Eichmann's indifference to the Holocaust. Though not as evil as the Holocaust itself, it was far more evil than any pleasures and achievements in his life, such as running the camp trains efficiently, were good. In fact, it was so evil that it made his life as a whole far more evil than good, or one it would have been vastly better not to live.

Admittedly, an attitude can sometimes seem more important than its object. If you go out of your way to cause me a minor pain, your petty malice may seem worse than the hurt it causes. If you make special efforts to give me a small pleasure, your benevolence can seem better than its effect. (Of gift giving we say, "It's the thought that counts.") But in these cases your goal is trivial, and when an attitude has a weightier object, such as students' knowledge or a torture victim's pain, its value is clearly less than its object's. When aimed at significant goods and evils, virtue and vice are lesser values.

This has an important implication for attitudes toward your own virtue. Let's say you're the teacher who teaches from a benevolent desire that her students gain knowledge. Just as an observer should be more pleased that your students learned than that you acted virtuously, you too should care more about the students' knowledge. If you instead care more about your virtue, you're being excessively self-concerned. Though your benevolent attitude is good, it's not as good as its object and therefore shouldn't be your primary focus. To make it primary is to exhibit a vice of disproportion, more specifically of priggishness or moral narcissism. Virtue involves caring appropriately about *other* goods and evils, and a fully virtuous person's attention is therefore directed mostly outward at those other values rather than inward at her own state of mind.

Priggishness is often a part of moral pride. This is the vice of caring too much about your own moral virtue, which you can do both in comparison to other people's virtue and in comparison to your virtue's objects. When you care more about your own excellence in helping others than about their being helped, you're not being excellent.

The same disproportion is found in the trait of sentimentality or kitsch as analyzed by Milan Kundera in his novel *The Unbearable Lightness of Being*. Kundera describes a U.S. senator who, trying to impress a visitor with the greatness of America, points to four children running across the grass and says,

"Just look at them. Now, that's what I call happiness." Kundera comments:

> Kitsch causes two tears to flow in quick succession. The first tear says: How nice to see children running on the grass! The second tear says: How nice to be moved, together with all mankind, by children running on the grass! It is the second tear that makes kitsch kitsch.

Kundera's second tear involves, again, an excessive concern with your own attitudes: you focus more on your own emotion than on what you're emoting about. This often distracts you from your initial object's banality; in the senator's case, what the children are doing isn't that wonderful, but he's too caught up in his own reaction to it to notice. But its root is the same focus inward rather than outward at the world and the greater goods it contains. Sentimentality may not be the most serious vice, but it still involves a double disproportion: caring too much about objects that don't merit it because you care too much about your own caring for them.

That virtue is a lesser good doesn't mean it has no value. Though less good than its object, a virtuous attitude can nonetheless be better than many of the pleasures and achievements you could have if you were less morally admirable. A life in which you're braver and more benevolent can be better even if it's less happy and achieves fewer goals. To be sad at a world of suffering, and therefore sad overall, is better than to maliciously delight in it or not care about it at all.

But there's a limit to virtue's value. If you stay virtuously loyal to your political movement's goals while being tortured by an oppressive regime, your virtue is good but not as good as your pain is evil. If all that lies ahead of you is more torture, it would be better for you not to live; like Eichmann's, though for the opposite reason, your future promises more evil than good. And only a high-minded philosopher could say otherwise.

FURTHER READINGS

The idea that virtue consists in loving independently given goods and hating independent evils is found in Hastings Rashdall, *The Theory of Good and Evil*, vol. 1, chaps. 3, 7; G. E. Moore, *Principia Ethica*, chap. 6; and W. D. Ross, *The Right and the Good*, chaps. 5, 7. I discuss it at greater length in my *Virtue, Vice, and Value*. A philosophically more influential but in my view less illuminating account of virtue is given in Aristotle's *Nicomachean Ethics*, especially bks. 2–4. Immanuel Kant affirms the supreme value of conscientiousness in sec. 1 of his *Groundwork of the Metaphysics of Morals*, while the example of the friend who visits only because it's her duty comes from Michael Stocker's "The Schizophrenia of Modern Ethical Theories." John Henry Newman prefers the destruction of all humanity to a single venial sin in *Certain Difficulties Felt by Anglicans in Catholic Teaching*, W. D. Ross makes a similar claim about the supreme value of virtue in *The Right and the Good*, chap. 6, and I defend the contrary view that virtue is a lesser good in *Virtue, Vice, and Value*, chap. 5.

Chapter Seven

LOVE AND FRIENDSHIP

All you need is love.

—The Beatles

Many of us can't imagine a good life without love. We may think mainly here of romantic or sexual love, the kind that can sweep you away and often leads to marriage and the raising of children. But there's also the non-erotic love we feel for our parents, children, and siblings and our affection for our friends—these too are forms of love. It may be too much to call love an essential good; maybe a life without it but with enough knowledge, achievement, and other sources of happiness can be well worth living. But for many of us loving and being loved are deeply desirable.

In this chapter I'll explore why love is good, what we love people for, and when if ever it should end. I'll treat the different forms of love, for a romantic partner, family member, or friend, as sufficiently similar to be species of a single genus. The forms differ, obviously, in their intensity: romantic love is more consuming than affection for a friend, which is in turn stronger than liking for an acquaintance. But they share key elements. You want to spend time with a lover and delight in her company, but the same is true to a lesser degree of a friend or even an acquaintance. The desire isn't as passionate in the last cases nor the time together so thrilling, but there's a similar urge toward togetherness. You also want a lover's happiness and do what you can to promote it; likewise, again to a lesser degree, with a friend. And you want both a lover's and a friend's success and personal development.

Of course romantic love has special aspects, like a desire to enjoy sexual pleasure with a partner and give that pleasure to her. But these are just specific forms of the desires to be with another and promote her happiness, which are likewise present in friendship—a difference again of degree, not kind. Romantic love also has a distinctive basis, often another's physical appearance or even smell, whereas the root of friendship is usually shared interests, and the foundation of love for a child is just the fact that he's yours. But what develops in all these cases has the same main elements: wanting to be with another and enjoy her company, and wanting her to be happy and achieve the other goods of life.

Love's praises have been sung in poems and pop songs; it's prompted some of the world's greatest art. But it's also been the subject of some very silly philosophy. Perhaps awed by the artists, philosophers have made overblown claims about love: that there's only one person in the world you can love, that in sexual arousal you're really responding to another's moral virtue, or that in sex two lovers create a fused being, dissolving the metaphysical boundaries between them. But appreciating love's value doesn't require these extravagances. It can be true that "love is a many-splendored thing" and "the greatest of these is love," even though love embodies familiar human values and arises in ordinary and even accidental ways.

A MANY-SPLENDORED THING

What makes love so valuable? It needn't be something distinctive of love and found nowhere else—love can just embody other, more basic goods to a high degree. And surely it does.

Most obviously, love can make you feel good. Shared erotic love involves the physical pleasures of sex, and all our attachments give us pleasures-that: that your friend got a promotion, that your child learned to walk, and, very centrally, that you yourself are loved. Love can also put you in a good mood—think of Gene Kelly "singin' in the rain"—and give you life satisfaction. How can you not feel good about your life when the person you want most loves you and is showing her love for you now?

Love also involves knowledge, since the people you love are usually the ones you understand best in the world. What you know about them may not be that extended, but it's internally connected, combining the different aspects of their lives into a single picture, and it's also explanatory and precise. Knowing a friend's specific abilities, for example, you understand why she's succeeded in business but has trouble sticking to a diet.

Love is also a site of achievement. In a long-term relationship you can help a partner realize goals not just now but into the future, such as that she finish her Ph.D. or stay active in theater. In the closest relationships you pursue goals that involve you both, such as to raise children or jointly design a house, and that involve many varied subgoals. And through all this you achieve more precisely with a loved one: you know just where to massage her to make her feel good or what exact words will lift her spirits.

Most important, love is where you're most virtuous. A key moral virtue is wanting other people's good: wanting their happiness, achievement, and even virtue. And though we should want these things for everyone, we want them most for those we care about. We take more pleasure in their pleasure and do more to further their goals; their pains pain us more, and their successes give us more joy. In much of our lives we're selfish, focused mainly on our own pleasures and goals, but love takes us out of ourselves, making us care about some people as much as we should care about everyone, so we're benevolent and compassionate in part of our life even if not in it all.

And this extra concern is itself virtuous, because it's proportionate. Your connection to a loved one makes her happiness, knowledge, and so on greater goods from your point of view than the same states in others, so you *should* care about them more. If she's depressed and a stranger is a little more depressed, you ought to comfort her first; if you don't, you fail in a special duty you owe her as someone you love. When two people love each other, their well-being has greater value from each other's point of view than a stranger's does, so each should care about the other's more, and their doing so, as long as it's not to excess, is good.

So are some other extra concerns in love. Just as you have a stronger duty to promote a loved one's good, so you have stronger duties not to lie to her, break promises to her, or interfere with her freedom. However wrong it is to do one of these things to a stranger, it's worse to do it to your partner; if you lie to her, she can ask not only "How could you do that?" but "How could you do that *to me*?" Now, most of us are more averse to violating these duties with a loved one, or find it more repellent; since our love strengthens the duties, that's again proportionate and good.

We shouldn't exaggerate the virtuous side of love, for our attachments are usually partly self-centered. Though you want someone you love to be happy, you especially want her to be happy *with you*; you wouldn't prefer her to be a little happier if that meant being made happy by someone else. This is clearest in erotic love: you want her to get sexual pleasure from you, not from whoever can best provide her with it.

This truth is often denied in sentimental fiction. In Charles Dickens's *A Tale of Two Cities*, Sydney Carton loves Lucie and takes the place on the guillotine of the man she loves, so that she can marry and be happy with that man. Carton wants Lucie to be happy even if it won't be with him, and he does what will secure her happiness even at the cost of his life. But most of us couldn't do that; we'd mostly want Lucie to be happy with us, getting pleasure from our love and our company.

Nor should we think there's virtue only in long-term relationships. Though it may be most fully present there, it can also be found in casual encounters. Two strangers can meet in a café and exchange life stories: if each is moved by the other's tale, they care virtuously about each other even though they may never meet again. The same is possible between casual sexual partners. If each wants the other's pleasure and is a genuinely generous lover, their coupling can be benevolent even if it's only for one night.

So love involves many goods—happiness, knowledge of another person, joint achievements, and virtuous desire for her good—and these often reinforce each other. If someone whose company you like also likes yours, you can get the pleasure of sharing time with her while benevolently giving the same pleasure to her. If the two of you pursue a joint goal, you can learn more about her in the process. But things aren't always this easy; sometimes the goods of love pull you in different directions.

If you love someone, you both want the pleasure of her company and want her to succeed in her career. But if she's offered a promotion in a faraway city, these two desires conflict and you can be torn between them. Or consider virtue and knowledge. Just as we engage in wishful thinking about ourselves, thinking we're better than we are, we do the same for loved ones. You want someone you care about to be smart, successful, and virtuous, and what you want her to be you often persuade yourself she is.

At the 1988 Summer Olympics Ben Johnson won the 100-meter sprint but then tested positive for steroids—it was an international scandal. When reporters contacted his sister for her reaction, she said, "I know my brother. Ben doesn't do drugs." This was on one hand a strange claim—wasn't there a positive test? But imagine that she'd said, "I've been giving Ben the benefit of the doubt, but this evidence is pretty damning. I guess he's a cheat." While rational, that wouldn't have been very sisterly, and people would have found it disloyal: shouldn't a sister believe in her brother? That's because part of love is having faith, or letting your desire for a loved one's good make you believe, even against your evidence, that he's what you want him to be. It may not give you knowledge, but it does show virtue.

There can be other conflicts in love. If a close friend is about to choose a career or romantic partner that you know will make her unhappy, your desire for her well-being may make you want to interfere: only by doing so can you stop her from hurting herself. But your respect for her freedom will make you want to let her decide for herself. And the conflict will be especially sharp because both emotions are stronger for someone you love: you want her happiness more than you want a stranger's, and you're more averse to restricting her choice. Kant said friendship involves a tension between love as a force of attraction that draws two people together and respect as a force of repulsion that keeps them apart; he concluded that perfect friendship is impossible. This last isn't news—who thought perfect anything is possible? But Kant did see how two admirable sides of friendship can pull us in different directions: one toward another person and into her life and the other away from her and out of her hair.

But these conflicts just follow if love is many-splendored. Our personal relationships add so much to our lives because they embody many goods at once, and sometimes these goods conflict, causing dilemmas that are wrenching because the emotions involved are so strong. Worse, sometimes the very features that make love wonderful make it a curse.

If someone you love rejects you or a cherished person dies, you can suffer anguish as deep as any you ever feel; here love causes suffering rather than joy. A romantic frenzy can blind you to a partner's major faults or make you squander your talents—it can ruin your life. And it can prompt not virtue but jealousy, possessiveness, and, in the worst case, hatred. What's a blessing at its best can be a blight when it fails.

But despite these dangers, few of us can resist love's lure; despite knowing its risks, we still find ourselves "taking a chance on love." It can hurt and it can harm, but for most of us love's glories are worth the gamble.

I LOVE YOU FOR A HUNDRED THOUSAND REASONS

In love the many elements of your emotion are directed at one person. You want and get pleasure from *her* company, know *her* better, and want *her* happiness more than other people's. There's a more impersonal kind of love that wants what's good for all people, but it's not our subject here, which is love for a particular individual. But how does it fix on her? What makes you love that person, and what do you love her for?

Partly—though, I'll argue, only partly—you love her for qualities other people could in principle share. You love her for her smile, for the way she makes you laugh, for her kindness to strangers and passion for the environment. She's not the only person whose jokes amuse you or who loves the wilderness, but she has those traits, and you love her for them. But they're of two types: some you admire, and some you just like.

You admire a quality if you think it's intrinsically good and would make anyone's life more desirable. Thus you can admire your love's wit or learning, or her dedication to a political cause. And if you're attracted by these qualities, you don't think that's a quirk in you; you think everyone should admire wit and dedication. But when you merely like a quality you don't have that thought. If you like her smile, for example, you don't think it's a better smile than any other or the one everybody should prefer; you just find yourself liking it. Or if you enjoy her company more than other people's, you needn't think her style of socializing superior to all others. You can realize that other people prefer different ways of spending time and wouldn't like her company best—but you just do.

So some of your love's qualities you'll admire, others you'll just like, and for some you'll do both. Thus, you may both admire and like the way she talks about movies or stays upbeat in tough times. But is one of these attitudes a better basis for love?

Philosophers who've discussed love often give primacy to admiration, as if the basis of an attachment should always be thoughts about another person's merits. Aristotle, for example, distinguished three types of friendship: ones of utility, based on how someone's useful to you; ones of pleasure, based on enjoying his company; and ones of virtue, based on admiring his moral character. He thought friendships of utility were the least good type and friendships of virtue the best: ideal friends would admire each other's moral virtues and love each other mainly for those virtues.

But this is far too high-minded. What's wrong with just liking someone? Aristotle assumed that in a friendship of utility or pleasure what you really want is just your own good. If you like someone because he's fun company, you really like him only as a means to your own enjoyment, which means you don't like him for himself and aren't really his friend at all. But this doesn't follow. The fact that you like someone's company can make you want his happiness, success, and even virtue as ends in themselves and not just as means to your pleasure; in fact, this often happens. You like someone first for partly selfish reasons, but then come to care for him altruistically. What's valuable in love is the desires and emotions it involves once it's developed, and those are largely independent of its origin. Beautiful flowers can bloom in everyday soil.

Aristotle recognized that friendship involves more than admiration, which can be given from afar and without ever meeting a person. He therefore envisaged friends living together and exercising their virtue jointly, pursuing shared moral projects and helping develop each other's characters. Again, though, why must specifically moral projects be central to the relationship? Why must working together at the food bank or in political campaigns be friends' main shared activity and seeing movies, traveling, and even sex just secondary?

I'm not saying you should love someone who's morally vicious, though that can happen between a parent and child. (Parental love can ignore traits that in any but a son or daughter would be repellent.) Maybe outside the family being morally decent is an essential condition of meriting your love, so you should befriend only people above a threshold of virtue. The question is why, beyond that, virtue must be the main basis of love, so what attracts you to someone is above all her moral qualities. It's not just that this isn't normal, that we're more often drawn to someone by her interests, by her appearance, or just because she's fun. It's that there's no reason why a relationship with that basis has to be second-rate. Aristotle's emphasis on virtue as a ground of love makes love more moralized and even prissy than it needs to be.

This is especially true of erotic love, where we're partly attracted by another's body, or by what philosophers coyly call her beauty. Here some philosophers have said that when we're aroused by someone's body we're really responding to it as the outer manifestation of her inner goodness or moral virtue. But now things are getting ridiculous. Are fashion models necessarily moral paragons? Is acne a sign of moral vice? One philosopher has said that we respond to another's body as the physical expression of her Kantian rational will, or her faculty of acting on the moral law. To which one can only say: there are a lot of rational-will sites on the Internet.

Our capacity for sexual arousal is implanted in us biologically. It's shared with other animals and reacts, as animals do, to purely physical features of a potential partner such as his face, body, and smell. In full-blown romantic love it's joined with attraction to other qualities, such as another's talents and moral character, to make a rich and complex whole. But it's always there, as a purely physical, purely sensual element. And its being there as purely sensual in no way detracts from the value of the love that results. As splendid as love is, it can spring partly from simple animal lust.

I LOVE YOU MOST OF ALL BECAUSE YOU'RE YOU

Let's say you love your partner for certain qualities: her wit, hair, and concern for the environment. Unless you're completely besotted, you don't think she has these qualities to the highest degree on the planet. She's not the single wittiest human nor does she have the one best hairstyle. If you think about it, you'll recognize that for any quality you love in her, there are some people who have it to a higher degree—for example, are more environmentally concerned. Even taking her qualities as a package, there are some who have a better version. If you meet one of these people, should you switch your love? Won't the new person have more of what you find loveable? You won't (I hope) do this; it would be horribly promiscuous.

Or consider a more radical example: your partner is dying and you're feeling devastated by the coming loss, but clever scientists tell you not to worry. They've extracted her DNA and are creating a clone who'll look exactly like her and have all her inborn qualities. Will you be comforted by this news and feel perfectly happy after the replacement? Surely not.

Maybe you worry that the clone won't have the qualities your partner gained during her life, such as the little scar over her eye and her intimate knowledge of you. But the scientists can handle that too. They've got a scanner that will produce a perfect molecular duplicate of her, including all her acquired traits and even memories. The duplicate will be indistinguishable from the original; if you weren't told about the switch you wouldn't know it had happened. But if you are told, will you think you've lost nothing by your partner's death? Again, surely not.

These examples show that while we love people partly for qualities others could share, we also love them as individuals, or for themselves. But what exactly does that mean?

One picture is that beneath all someone's qualities is the real person, the one who has the qualities, and that's what you love. It's the person with the wit and hair that you love, not the wit and hair themselves. But what is this real person like? She has to be completely featureless: no personality (that's a quality), no physical appearance, no memories, no nothing. At best she's like a clear Lucite globe to which her qualities attach. But how can you love a Lucite globe? And how can you love one of them rather than another, hers rather than Madonna's, if they're all indistinguishable? Talk of a real underlying self leads quickly to absurdity.

There's a more straightforward explanation of what it means to love someone as an individual. It's still to love her for qualities, but for ones that no one else could share. It's to love her for historical qualities, involving her participation with you in a shared past. You've done things together and affected each other in countless ways, and you can love her for those historical facts: for that nervous first meeting for drinks, for the time you sang together in the car, for the way she welcomed you home from France. And later you can love her for how the two of you bought a house, raised children, and matured and aged together.

These are still qualities, though historical ones. Or if that sounds odd, they're properties—things that are true of her—that you can love her for having. But they're also properties that, once she's had them, no one else can have. Someone else can be wittier or have better hair, but once she had those first drinks with you, no one else can be the person who did that then. A clone can't, nor can a molecular duplicate. The duplicate will have something like memories of the drinks: she can describe what happened and how it felt, even laugh with you about it. But they won't be real memories, and the duplicate won't be the person who really was there. And that's the person you love.

Of course a past takes time to develop. If you've just met identical twins, you can't love one of them more than the other. It's only when you've spent time with one and started to develop a history with her that you can care more about her than about her sister. Nor will just any shared history do; it has to be of the right kind. A past involving mutual hostility isn't a basis for love; if anything, it can make you hate someone more than you do people with the same non-historical qualities. You have to have shared good experiences with someone, ones that were pleasurable or rewarding. Once you've had those experiences, however, they're a further basis for love beyond qualities that others can share, like her wit and hair.

This attachment via history isn't something we feel only for people. I love my living-room furniture partly because it's a beautiful example of twentieth-century modernist design, but also because it's the furniture my father bought in the 1940s and that I grew up with. There may be more beautiful furniture, even in the same style, but I want to live with these chairs and these bookcases. You can keep wearing a ratty sweater or driving a wonky car because you've done things and gone places in it for such a long time. A friend of mine kept a pencil eraser for forty-four years; it was worn down and hard to use, but he wouldn't trade it for another. He wanted *that* pencil eraser. The people we love are more complex than pencil erasers, but when we're attached to them as individuals we love them in the same historical way, or for the same past role in our lives.

THROUGH THE YEARS MY LOVE WILL GROW

Love inevitably changes through time, at its best in ways that preserve and enhance its value. The philosopher C. D. Broad described this process beautifully: "If we may compare prolonged and successful sexual love for a person to the course of a river from its source to the sea, it begins as a violent torrent in a narrow bed full of rocks and shallows; in its middle it receives many tributaries; and in its later stages it becomes a calm wide deep stream." But there are different ways love can change.

One is in its shared activities. Writing in the 1920s, Broad thought sex would be much less important to a middle-aged couple than when they were young. (Tell that to the baby boomers.) But some changes like this happen, with, say, gardening replacing late-night clubbing as what two people most like to do.

Love's basis can also change, starting on its historical side. Over time you and your partner come to have shared more experiences: not just that first nervous meeting, but also the clubbing and then the gardening and the raising of children. So one way the river of love can deepen is by adding more, and more important, historical connections.

But you can also come to love a partner for new non-historical properties. (Broad suggests this in his talk of "tributaries," which have independent sources.) Maybe you always valued patience, didn't at first realize how patient she is, and now love her for that trait. Or you didn't value patience but learned to treasure it by observing hers. Or the two of you changed together. When you were young, she was impetuous and you loved impetuousness; then the same process that changed your interests from clubbing to gardening made her more patient and you more appreciative of patience.

Often, though, these changes are historically driven. Having first liked your love's wit and hair, you now treasure others among her qualities, such as her throaty laugh and fondness for snow. Did you think in the abstract about these qualities and decide, independently of who has them, that they're loveable? Or do you love them because they're hers? Surely the latter. You liked her first for some non-historical qualities, then developed a past with her and loved her for her part in it, and later came to love others of her qualities because they're hers. You love the throaty laugh because it's the laugh of the person you did those things with, though if she had a tinkly giggle you'd love that instead. A Gershwin brothers song relishes "the way you wear your hat / the way you sip your tea." The singer didn't first admire those ways of handling hats and teacups and then notice his lover using them; he first loved her and then loved them as things she did.

This explains why love can survive the loss of the qualities that ignited it. Though you first loved your partner for her smooth skin and slender waist, it's now thirty years later and she has wrinkles and a thickening middle. Do you stop loving her? Not at all. You now love her wrinkles and find them beautiful because they belong to someone you did important things with. Having once loved her for her appearance, you now love her appearance for being hers.

So your history with a loved one plays two roles. Added to an initial attraction to qualities others can share, it makes you love her for things others can't share and so to love her as an individual. But it also gives you new non-historical qualities to love her for. Traits you might not be attracted to in themselves you come to cherish as belonging to her.

This makes even more true something that already was true: that though you love just one person now and won't accept substitutes, there are many other people you could have loved. This isn't the romantic view, which says there's only one person in the world you can truly love, one who's "meant" for you. In Plato's *Symposium*, the speaker Aristophanes says we were all originally joined with another person to form a globular sphere; Zeus then cut us in two, and ever since we've been seeking our other half because only with him or her can we feel whole. The same idea is expressed in dating-site profiles that say "looking for my soul mate."

But again this isn't credible. (If there's just one person in the world you can love, how come she so often goes to your high school?) It also isn't necessary. That your love is now focused on one person doesn't mean it has to have been intended for her in advance. And there are many ways you could have loved someone different.

Consider the initial qualities that attracted you: your love's wit, hair, and environmental concern. There are other people in the world who have the same qualities to a higher degree, and if you'd met one of them first you might well have loved her instead. Different qualities could also have done the trick. Though you were attracted by one person's wit and hair, you could equally well have liked another's empathy and smooth skin. Most of us aren't so undiscriminating that we can be attracted by any set of qualities, but not so picky that it has to be just one.

And whoever initially attracted you, you would have developed a history with her and then loved her for being part of it. You wouldn't have loved her for nervous first drinks and singing in a car; it might instead have been a walk by the lake and a weekend in Montreal. But you'd have loved her as the unique person who did those things with you, and you again wouldn't have accepted a substitute, not even a molecular duplicate. Loving her historical qualities would also have made you love other qualities because they were hers: if not a throaty laugh, then a tinkly giggle. At the end you would have loved her as a unique individual, but with a different starting point the process would have ended with you loving someone different.

In fact, even ideal love can have an entirely accidental origin. Maybe if you'd gone to a different bar that night, or had one more or less drink, you wouldn't have ended up loving the person you did. No matter: those events, however contingent, started a process that led to your loving her now. And, whatever its origin, that love is now wonderful.

The philosopher René Descartes thought there has to be as much value or reality in a thing's cause as in the thing itself: something as great as our idea of God must have an equally great origin, such as God himself. But often something very good or bad results from trivial causes combined in the right way. It was an accident—a fluke of timing and mood and alcohol—that you started building a history with this person rather than with any of hundreds of others. But from that accident has come the splendid affection you now share.

WHEN A LOVELY FLAME DIES

If love often starts in accident, how does it end? Should it ever end, or is the best love forever? The romantic view is that true love never dies, that, as Shakespeare put it, "love is not love / which alters when it alteration finds." But unfortunately sometimes there are good reasons for love to die.

You love a partner for historical qualities she can't lose but also for non-historical ones she can. And though you love some of the latter only because they're hers, you like or admire others independently. If she retains all these last qualities, your love can persist and deepen, but what if she loses some?

If they're only minor qualities, your love needn't change: she still has many other loveable traits. It would be utterly shallow if, having been attracted to her partly for her hair, you dump her because she's changed its style. But other non-historical qualities are more important. Maybe you were first attracted by her concern for the environment and willingness to fight for those less fortunate, but then she changed. Having gone into law to help the poor, she's ended up at a corporate firm, caring most about the money she earns. She still has other engaging qualities as well as her role in your past, so you give her time to rethink her priorities. But if the change in her values becomes permanent, won't that be a reason to reconsider your love? Can't you say the person you once loved no longer exists?

This example involves moral qualities (the philosophers' favorite), but others can play a similar role. Maybe you initially loved her wit and vitality, but since then she's lost her sparkle and became a couch potato. This isn't exactly a moral failing; you didn't admire her liveliness so much as like it. But isn't it still a reason to reconsider your tie? It certainly is with friends. Our attachments to them depend largely on enjoying their company, and when that fades so does friendship. The issue is harder with romantic love, which has a more complex basis, including a richer shared history. But there too, the loss of qualities you just like, such as being fun company, can erode your attachment.

Or the change can be in you. Whereas you once loved your partner's impetuousness, you've come to prefer patience; what you once found charming in her now seems flaky. Or your history with her can change. What were once enjoyable interactions can become mundane or even hostile—think of a marriage gone bad. And if only a good past gives you reason to love someone, a bad one does the opposite. Your partner may be the person you had those nervous first drinks with, but she's also the one who just said she hates you and with whom you had that horrible last fight. Broad recognized this possibility: after describing the river of successful love he added, "Too often, of course, there is no such happy ending, and the stream peters out into the shallows of mere habitual toleration or the swamps of mutual irritation and frustration."

The idea that love should last forever makes a relationship's initial history paramount over all its other aspects: if its first interactions were good, it doesn't matter what non-historical qualities your partner has acquired since or how awful your more recent history with her has been. But this ignores the complexity of love's foundations.

Love is many-splendored not only because it embodies many different goods but also because it has many bases. You can love a person for physical, moral, and emotional qualities, and you can love her for her distant as well as more recent past with you. While this multiplicity adds to the richness of love, it also increases the ways it can fail, or the number of its foundations that can break down. If enough do, the structure may rightly crumble.

Your history with a loved one is important and will often make you respond to changes in her by loving her new qualities because they're hers. But that can only go so far; sometimes people grow too far apart. Friendships end, and 41 percent of American first marriages end in divorce. It's sad when it happens, and in many cases it could have been avoided. But when you love someone it's for who she is and what she's done. If she or her history with you changes enough, your love can and sometimes should die.

FURTHER READINGS

The idea that love is not a distinctive value but combines other goods such as pleasure, knowledge, and virtue is suggested in W. D. Ross, *The Right and the Good*, chap. 5. Kant claims that friendship involves a conflict between love and respect in a section on friendship in his *Doctrine of Virtue*, while Aristotle discusses the three types of friendship in *Nicomachean Ethics*, bks. 8–9. I discuss the historical basis of love in "The Justification of National Partiality" and *Virtue, Vice, and Value*, chap. 7; C. D. Broad's quote about successful sexual love comes from his *Examination of McTaggart's Philosophy*.

Chapter Eight

PUTTING IT TOGETHER

Bend me, shape me . . .

—The Outsiders

A main theme of this book has been that there isn't just one intrinsic good but many, not just pleasure or virtue but also knowledge, achievement, and maybe more. And each of these goods has several forms: not only physical pleasure but also life satisfaction and a good mood, knowing your inner self as well as scientific laws, living a unified life and completing a single difficult task.

This means there isn't one life that's best for everyone— not the gourmet's or the philosopher's but many different good lives suited to different people's talents and situation. You can live well as a scientist, as a dancer, or by caring for others in your family and neighborhood; you can pursue knowledge or live for achievement. It's not that any life is equally good: some are clearly better than others. But the better ones can have very different contents.

How good a life is depends, first, on the individual good things it contains: its individual pleasures, items of understanding, and so on. But it also depends on two more factors. One is how the different goods compare in value with each other. How much goodness does pleasure contribute to your life as against knowledge? Is it better to be happier but a little callous, or sadder and more compassionate? Is doing better than thinking?

The other factor is your life's overall shape. You can aim for a well-rounded achievement of many goods or concentrate mostly on one. Is either of these preferable? How about a life of radical ups and downs versus one at a consistently moderate level? And is a longer life always better?

These are all questions about how the total value in your live arises from the individual good things it contains. Let's take them in turn.

COMPARING GOODS

I've already made some suggestions about how different values compare. One is that pleasure is less good than pain is evil, in part because the value of extra pleasure gets less the more pleasure you have; though more pain is always very bad, more pleasure isn't always very good. If that's so, however, then past a point pleasure should also have less value than other goods, and that seems right. It can be worth giving up significant knowledge or achievement to avoid agony, but not to move from ecstasy to even greater bliss.

I've also said that a virtuous attitude has less value than its object does, so compassion for another's pain is less good than her pain is evil. This makes virtue in one sense a lesser good, but it can still make a significant contribution to your life. The best attitudes are directed at major values outside yourself, such as relief for many people's pain, and something that's less good than one of these objects can be better than many pleasures or items of knowledge in you. Certainly malice or selfishness can outweigh the goodness in your life of much happiness or achievement.

These suggestions haven't, I confess, been very precise. I haven't said exactly how quickly the value of extra pleasure diminishes or just what fraction of its object's value a virtuous attitude has. But this is just inevitable: we can never compare values more than vaguely, as becomes even clearer when we consider other pairs such as knowledge and achievement.

Compare one life devoted to learning about the history of the twentieth century and another spent running a medium-sized business. Can we say that either is clearly better? I don't see how: neither the knowledge in the first nor the achievement in the second seems plainly superior, yet they also aren't exactly equal in value. We can say the two lives are in the same general range of value, or roughly on a par, but we can't say anything more definite.

This isn't because we can never compare knowledge and achievement. Successfully running a business is better than knowing how many bullets were fired at the Battle of the Somme; knowing everything about World War I is better than selling a single widget. But in intermediate cases like the one above we can't decisively compare the two goods, and the same holds for other pairs such as knowledge and pleasure. Understanding World War I is better than enjoying a single chocolate, but compared to a decade of delicious meals? It seems impossible to say.

This may be disappointing—shouldn't philosophy answer all our questions? But the fact that values can be only vaguely compared reinforces the idea that there are many good lives. If the goods could all be precisely compared, there might be different best lives for different people but a single best life for each: one precise combination of pleasure, knowledge, and so on that best suited his talents and situation. But if that's not so, there may be several lives available to each person that are roughly equally good, with none better than the rest. Isn't that our situation: that we can recognize some lives we could lead as better but none as uniquely best?

This is even more true if the value of one good relative to another isn't constant but can vary from context to context—which is precisely what it does if a life's value also depends on its shape, or on how it combines its elements into a package. That's our next topic.

THE WELL-ROUNDED LIFE

Here are two ways to organize your life. In one you seek a well-rounded achievement of all the goods: pleasure, knowledge, achievement, virtue, all at a reasonably high level but also in a certain proportion or balance. (In practice, this means spending roughly equal time on each.) And you do the same for each good on its own, seeking a mix of the types of pleasure and of achievements in many fields, such as business, poetry, and golf. Your aim isn't just the greatest total of the intrinsic goods, but a balanced variety of them all.

The alternative is to focus on one good and make your achievement of that as great as possible. You live almost exclusively for pleasure or knowledge or, in the realm of achievement, concentrate on business and ignore everything else. Here you don't seek breadth or balance; you want your life's single best element to be the best it can be.

Of these two lives, I think many people will find the first, well-rounded one more attractive. It fits the ideal of the "Renaissance man" typified by Leonardo da Vinci, with his varied accomplishments in painting, science, and engineering, and explains our admiration for those who add a career in politics to one in art or sports, such as Benjamin Disraeli (novelist and prime minister) and Bill Bradley (basketball star and senator).

A well-rounded life has also appealed to philosophers. Wilhelm von Humboldt thought we should aim at "the highest and most harmonious development of [our] powers to a complete and consistent whole," while Marx and Nietzsche railed against specialization and the division of labor. In Marx's utopia each person would be able "to do one thing today and another tomorrow, to hunt in the morning, fish in the afternoon, rear cattle in the evening, criticize after dinner, just as [he has] a mind," while Nietzsche mocked the "nook-dwellers" and "fragments of humanity" he found at European universities; for him a human's greatness lay in his "range and multiplicity, in his wholeness in manifoldness."

But if well-roundedness is an ideal, then the comparative values of, say, knowledge and achievement aren't always the same. If you've lived a mostly intellectual life, with more thinking than doing, it will do more to improve your life if you now try something active than if you learn more facts. But if the opposite is true—if you've been more active than intellectual—you'll gain more by adding some knowledge. In each case what you have less of has more value now.

This variability can be illustrated in a diagram. In Figure 8.1 the vertical axis represents the knowledge you have and the horizontal axis your achievement, while each curve represents combinations of knowledge and achievement that have equal value, with curves further out from the origin representing more value than ones closer in. Points *A* and *B* therefore have the same value as each other, as do the points on the next curve out, and the latter all have more value than either *A* or *B*.

What captures the ideal of well-roundedness here is that the curves *curve*; more specifically, they bulge in toward the

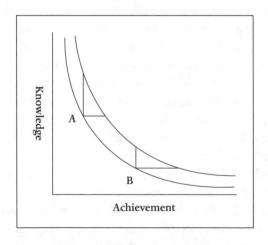

Figure 8.1

origin. If you're at point *A*, with lots of knowledge (you're fairly far up the vertical axis) but little achievement (you're not very far right), you can make the same improvement in your life by adding either a large amount of new knowledge (the thin line going up) or a small amount of achievement (the shorter line going right); each takes you to the same next curve. So here a little more achievement equals a lot more knowledge. But if you're at *B*, with much more achievement than knowledge, you can make the same improvement by adding either a little knowledge or a lot of achievement. In each case it's better to increase what you have less of, creating pressure to balance the goods.

But isn't well-roundedness a dangerous ideal? Can't seeking it leave you a jack of all trades and master of none? If you try to balance many goods, you can dissipate your energies and not achieve much in any; the result will be dilettantism and mediocrity. It would be wonderful to speak twenty languages, but if you try learning them all at once, you'll end up not speaking any well.

The objection here isn't to the ideal of well-roundedness as such, but only to its practicability. Even if goods matter more the less of them you have, aiming for balance will be counterproductive if it reduces the amount of each you achieve. You want both well-roundedness and a high level of all the goods, the objection says, but seeking the first goal will frustrate the second. For real value in any field you have to specialize.

Let's call the basis of this objection the dilettante's disadvantage. We can illustrate it in our diagrams by adding an option line representing the greatest combinations of knowledge and achievement possible for a person given her talents and situation; all the lives available to her are therefore on or below this line. In Figure 8.2 this line is straight and therefore touches the farthest-out curve, or has its most valuable point, right in its middle, where the knowledge and achievement it represents are equal. Here well-roundedness is indeed best. But our objection says that real-life option lines won't be straight. They too will bulge in toward the origin, so lives that try to balance the goods won't have much of either and well-roundedness shouldn't in practice be pursued.

But the dilettante's disadvantage isn't the only relevant factor, because there are also costs of concentration that can make specialization counterproductive. One of these costs is simply diminishing returns. If you've already studied World War I for eight hours today, how much will you gain from an extra hour? Wouldn't you do better to switch to a different activity? Moreover, in many activities it's easier to move from

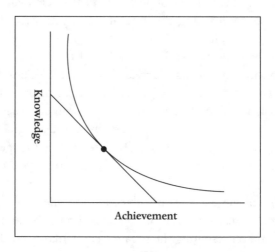

Figure 8.2

low to middling achievements than from there to the highest heights. In ballet it takes some effort to move from a beginner's level to the corps of an amateur production, but more to move from there to a professional troupe. At the highest levels, dancers practice for many hours to improve their technique a tiny bit. Finally, major advances in one field often come from applying insights drawn from a quite different field, for example, applying mathematics to soccer or game theory to biology. To do only one thing is to cut yourself off from such advances; in that respect to be narrow is to be worse in your own specialty.

So there are two opposing factors to consider: the dilettante's disadvantage, which makes the option line bulge inward and seeking well-roundedness unwise, and the costs of concentration, which do the opposite. But we may be able to combine them in a single picture, because they seem to work most powerfully at different levels.

The dilettante's disadvantage seems strongest at low levels of achievement and weaker higher up. In many fields you have to invest a lot of time before any significant value results: in an intellectual field you have to grasp basic concepts and principles and in a sport you need fundamental skills, and without these you can't accomplish much. Once you have these concepts or skills, however, you can use them to acquire more advanced ones, and for a time your progress is rapid. The pursuit of well-roundedness is therefore most counterproductive when it stops you from acquiring any fundamentals, as when trying to learn twenty languages leaves you knowing the grammar of none. But it's less harmful further along, when you're established in each of several pursuits and can progress simultaneously in them all.

The costs of concentration, by contrast, seem greatest at high levels of achievement. It's only when you've spent a lot of the day on history that spending more will be a waste; the same isn't true after one hour. And cross-fertilization happens mainly at high levels; it's only when you know a lot about both math and soccer that you can use one to illuminate the other.

Given all these facts, however, many people's option-lines may be M-shaped, as in Figure 8.3. In the top left and bottom right of this diagram, where your achievement of one good is high, the costs of concentration work strongly on that good to make the line slope steeply toward the axis, so putting more into that good will yield only limited gains. In the middle, however, where your achievement of both goods is lower, the disadvantage dominates and the line bulges in. The result is that you have two better lives available to you, each

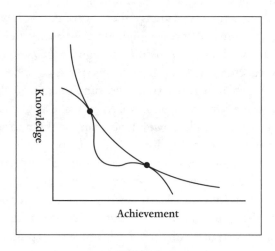

Figure 8.3

concentrating to some degree on one good. You should be neither a pure specialist nor a pure all-rounder, but give a moderate preponderance to one good over the other. A similar conclusion holds if we consider not just two but many goods. Then you may have several best lives you can live, each concentrating moderately on one good but including some attention to others. You may be mostly a thinker but also play some sports, or study mainly biology but have a lesser interest in history.

There's a further implication of these claims. If the dilettante's disadvantage is strongest at low levels and the costs of concentration are greatest higher up, this should affect not only individual option lines but also a sequence of lines representing the lives available to different people. For those with limited abilities or a short life span, the disadvantage should work powerfully on their options, creating a deep central trough in their lines. But for those with more talent or time this factor should be less important. As their lines move farther out from the origin, their troughs should become shallower and may even disappear, as in Figure 8.4. Then exceptional individuals like Leonardo and Disraeli can and should pursue many goods—they should lead Renaissance lives—while those of us with more limited gifts must content ourselves with being some kind of specialist. Well-roundedness can be a practicable ideal, but only for a select few.

How you should divide your time between different goods depends on two things: how their values compare with each other and which combinations of them you can actually achieve. An attractive view about the first issue favors well-roundedness, but a realistic view about the second usually does the opposite. For most of us, the best lives we can lead

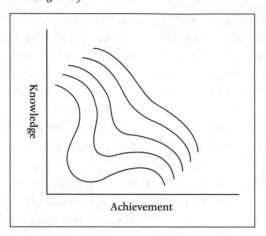

Figure 8.4

will concentrate moderately on one or a few goods. They'll be as rounded as we can manage, but to be more rounded is indeed to be mediocre.

LIFE'S UPS AND DOWNS

Your life has a shape not only in how it balances different goods but also in its trajectory through time, or from year to year. Its quality can go up, go down, or stay the same. Is one of these better than another? It's often hard to say.

Consider two lives of the same length and with the same total of all the goods, but with opposite trajectories through time. One life—*A* in Figure 8.5—starts out at a high level of quality but then steadily declines. The other—*B*—starts at a low level but improves; here you can truly say, "Every day, in

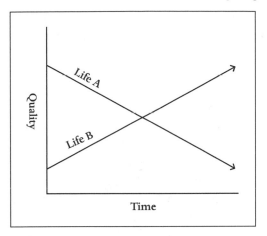

Figure 8.5

every way, I'm getting better and better." The two lives move in opposite directions—is one better?

I think many people will prefer the second life, saying it's in general better to be on an upward slope than a downward one. And that may be right—but we need to be careful.

Given how much we focus on changes in our situation, an improving life such as *B* will probably contain extra pleasures ("Today's better than yesterday!") while *A* will contain disappointments. And if you intentionally produced the improvements in *B*, it will also have extra achievements. To compensate, we may have to imagine *A* containing some additional pleasures, perhaps physical ones, and some additional achievements. Is it then so clear that it's less good?

In some careers, such as sports and mathematics, your greatest achievements typically come early in life. If you're a basketball star, you may later be a successful coach, but it's what you did on the court in your twenties that's most memorable; that age is also when mathematicians prove their most important theorems. But in careers such as politics your greatest achievements usually come much later; only then are you foreign secretary or prime minister with the opportunities those positions bring. An athlete's or mathematician's life is therefore closer to life *A* and a politician's to *B*. Does that make the politician's life better? I'm not sure it does, and even if it does, the difference surely isn't large.

Here's another contrast. Of two lives with the same total of the goods, one life—*A* in Figure 8.6—stays at a consistently moderate level while another, *B*, alternates between moments of great value and ones of low or even negative value. *A*'s shape is a flat plateau; *B*'s has tall peaks and deep valleys. Is one of them better?

An up-and-down life like *B* has more varied levels of good, but a constant life like *A* can be varied in its own way, with

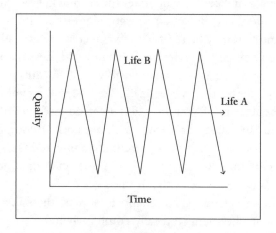

Figure 8.6

mostly knowledge at one time and mostly achievement at another. And though *A* lacks the pleasures of sudden improvement, which can make it seem less good, *A* also lacks the pains of drastic decline. Life *B* may be more interesting to watch; it may have more aesthetic appeal and would probably make a better movie. But it's not clear that this is relevant to its value in itself, or for the person who lives it. And is it really better to alternate between ecstasy and moderate pain than always to be reasonably content, or between saintly benevolence and moderate malice than just to be steadily virtuous? I don't see that it is.

Some think it's good if your life has a narrative shape, the kind found in a good play or novel. This means, first, that its elements are unified by all contributing to a single "plot," and, second, that this plot follows an aesthetically pleasing arc, for example, through rising action to a climax and then a denouement. The idea here is that it's good if your life is structured like a story.

When your life is organized around a single end, the connections that unify it are ones you intentionally created: you pursued these goals as means to that end. But the characters in a narrative needn't be aware of its unifying connections, which may be evident only to a reader. (Think of a Shakespeare play with a separate subplot that parallels and comments on its main plot.) But can connections of this kind really make your life better? Mustn't any unity that adds value be one you intentionally created?

As for a narrative arc, our lives do sometimes approximate to that. There's our long period of childhood when we acquire the tools for later achievements, then a peak period, and a final decline. But at least with respect to pleasure it's not clear that there's always rising action: isn't childhood among our very happiest times? And a normal life's denouement lasts far longer than a good drama would allow. *King Lear* has only fifteen more lines after its hero dies, but many people's retirement lasts for years.

And we again have to ask why a shape that's more pleasing to an observer should make a life better in itself—why is that relevant? Still, there's one point where something like narrative considerations may bear on your life's value. We encounter it when we stop holding the length of a life constant, as we've done till now, and ask whether it's always better to live a longer time.

MORE, MORE, MORE?

One benefit of medical science has been to extend the human life span. Not long ago the average life expectancy was around forty years, but now many people live into their eighties and even nineties. And we can imagine this process continuing, with science one day enabling people to live to 150 or even 200. But imagine that it does this without extending the period of their prime, so the added years are like those people now spend in their nineties, typically in a nursing home. These years aren't painful or in some other way bad in themselves, but they involve limited pleasures, minimal activity, and significantly reduced understanding. Would a hundred extra years like that make your life better?

Some people will say yes, thinking more years of positive quality always a plus. But isn't there a temptation to say no? Though the extra years aren't intrinsically bad, we may think, they're so far below the level of your prime that they'd make your life as a whole less good. An existence whose period of decline is so out of proportion to its time of highest achievement has a regrettable shape.

Or consider a more realistic example. You could either die at eighty-five or live another ten years with advanced Alzheimer's disease, barely aware of things around you and needing care in every aspect of your life. If you've been active and intelligent up to eighty-five, couldn't adding these years reduce your life's value?

We sometimes think this way about careers, especially in sports. Muhammad Ali was perhaps the greatest boxer ever, yet he extended his career well past its prime, especially in his last fights against Larry Holmes and Trevor Berbick. And many boxing fans think it would have been better if he had retired earlier. It's not that his later performances were by some neutral standard bad; for many another boxer, to do as well as Ali did against Holmes or Berbick would have marked the pinnacle of his career. But Ali's last fights were so far below his own peak that they made *his* career less good.

We can think similarly about artists. A poet could write a hundred exceptionally fine poems, or those plus two hundred mediocre poems. Wouldn't the second be less good? And would Kurt Cobain's musical career have been better if he'd lived into his fifties and become a lounge singer playing Las Vegas?

At least one philosopher has taken this view about human lives. Nietzsche urged us to "die at the right time," by which he meant neither too early nor, as he thought happened more often, too late: "One must cease letting oneself be eaten when one tastes best: that is known to those who want to be loved long. . . . All-too-many live, and all-too-long they hang on their branches." (Unfortunately, his last ten years were marked by mental illness, meaning Nietzsche's own life didn't live up to his ideal.)

Was Nietzsche right that in human lives more can be less? The issue is how we combine the goods in different years in a life into a measure of its overall value, especially when its number of years isn't fixed.

The simplest way is by adding, so the overall value in your life is just the sum of the goods it contains in every year. But then adding extra low-quality years does always make your life better; it even follows that adding a hundred years of nursing-home life can be better than adding ten years in your prime. So long as each nursing-home year is more than a tenth as good as each prime year, a century of them will do more to improve your life.

If that's hard to accept, we can equate your life's overall value with its average goodness per year; then extra years below your average do make it worse. But this goes too far in the opposite direction. Bobby Orr and Wayne Gretzky were the greatest hockey players ever, but while Gretzky played for twenty seasons, Orr's career was ended by injury after ten. If all that mattered were his average per year, Orr's career would be no worse for that fact.

There's an intermediate possibility. I've said that increases in your pleasure matter less the more pleasure you have; here we can say, analogously, that, given a fixed average goodness per year in your life, extra years add less value the more years you've lived (Figure 8.7). Then a longer life is always, other things equal, better, but adding a hundred low-quality years can be less good than adding ten prime ones. And past a point

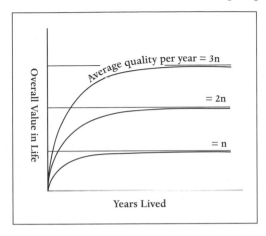

Figure 8.7

lower-quality years do make your life less good. They no longer add much value by lengthening your life, and they detract from it by lowering its average goodness per year, or dropping it to a lower curve in the diagram. Though not in themselves bad, extra years with advanced Alzheimer's can make your life worse.

Should we accept this intermediate view and, with Nietzsche, want to fall off our branches before we get over-ripe? The issue is difficult, and different factors can push us in different directions.

One factor is our age. I think younger people are more likely to prefer a shorter but higher-quality existence, or want to "live fast, die young, and leave a good-looking corpse." But those who are older may focus more on the specific goods ahead of them, the pleasures and achievements (albeit limited), and want the years that will make them possible.

Maybe they won't think about the overall shape of their life; maybe they will, and will prefer it with the addition. But I think those nearer the end of life are more likely to favor lower-quality extensions. (And middle-aged people? We may just be confused.)

Another factor is the kind of good we value most. Pleasure and happiness seem less friendly to the Nietzschean view because they aren't goods we usually think it can be bad to get more of. If the second week of a vacation will be slightly less enjoyable than the first, that's surely no reason to cancel it. Likewise for virtue. If you know you won't be quite as benevolent in later years—you'll get a little crotchety in old age—that's no reason to abandon virtue. Like pleasure, virtue seems a good it's always better to add to, even at lower levels.

Knowledge and achievement, by contrast, do invite the Nietzschean view. It's when your intellectual powers decline and the goals you once achieved become impossible that addition seems to subtract; it's with these goods that we most take the quasi-aesthetic attitude of preferring the shorter and higher-quality to the longer but lower-grade. It's therefore no accident that the main examples motivating the Nietzschean view are of careers in sports or art, where skill and achievement are to the fore.

So what we think of this view, and of lower-quality life extensions more generally, may depend on what we think matters more: pleasure and virtue on one side, or knowledge and achievement on the other. If we think the former are the greatest goods, we may welcome added years of lesser quality as improving our lives at least somewhat. If we prize the latter, we may think those years better not lived.

But this is just the issue—of how different goods compare—that we found so hard to resolve at the start of this chapter. And now it makes another issue, about the ideal length of your life, more difficult. But this seems, again, to be our situation. Philosophy can't always say decisively what makes for the best life. Sometimes it can only ask a question, describe possible answers to it, and leave each of us to resolve it on our own.

AND IN THE END . . .

The most important thing about your life's shape is that it ends—in death. That leaves a final question about whether dying is bad, and if so, why.

Epicurus and his followers in the ancient world thought dying isn't bad at all. Once you're dead, they argued, you can't suffer any evil; since you don't exist, you can't be harmed. There's therefore nothing to fear in death, and to do so is to cause yourself needless pain. Death should be nothing to you because it is, literally, nothing.

Epicurus combined this argument with a hedonistic view of what's good. He thought the only evil is pain, and that dying can't be bad because when you're dead you can't feel any pain. But the same is true of other evils. When you're dead you can't have malicious desires or false beliefs or fail to achieve important goals. You can't be in any bad state because you're not in any state at all.

Though Epicurus was right that death isn't bad in itself, it doesn't follow that dying isn't bad at all. Dying can be bad because of its effects. More specifically, it can be bad because it deprives you of goods you would otherwise have enjoyed. Let's say you're killed in a car accident at twenty-five. If the accident hadn't happened, you would have lived sixty more years full of happiness, understanding, and benevolence, and your death harms you because it prevents your life from containing those good things.

Nor is death alone in being bad as a deprivation. Imagine there was a terrific TV show on last night but you missed it because you fell asleep. Your sleeping wasn't bad in itself—it didn't hurt—nor did it cause anything bad. But it deprived you of the pleasure you would have got from watching the show. Dying can be bad in the same way, by preventing goods you would have enjoyed if only you'd lived.

But if this is why dying is bad, then it isn't always bad. If you have a painful terminal illness and only a week of suffering ahead of you, your dying now is positively good: it prevents evils rather than preventing goods. Likewise, if you're a captured spy facing torture, then taking a cyanide pill is a benefit. And if we accept Nietzsche's view, death can be good if it stops you from adding low-quality years to a previously high-quality life.

It also follows that the deaths that are bad aren't equally so. Someone who dies at eighty-five after a satisfying life doesn't lose as much as a twenty-five-year old who's killed in a car accident. There are fewer years he would otherwise have lived, and he's therefore deprived of less good by dying now.

Nor need death deprive you only of future goods. At twenty-five you'll have done many things to prepare for your life ahead. You'll have gone to college, say, to qualify for the veterinary career you always wanted. In a longer life these activities would have had value as parts of a successfully completed life plan; they would have been lower-down items in a hierarchy of achievements with a veterinary career on top. But if you die at twenty-five, that hierarchy never gets completed; its top goal never gets added on, and your preparatory activities have less value than if they'd served their ultimate aim.

Dying young is therefore not only a loss but a waste; things you've already done end up contributing less value to your life than they would have had you lived longer, so your death makes not only your future but also your past less good. As one philosopher said, "Earlier actions, preparations, planning, whose entire purpose lay in their being directed towards some future goal, become, in the face of an untimely death, retrospectively pointless—bridges, so to speak, that terminate in mid-air, roads that lead nowhere." This is another reason why dying at twenty-five is more tragic than dying at eighty-five. At eighty-five you won't have been making elaborate preparations for your future, so you won't have many earlier activities to be wasted. Not only does dying then cost you less future good, it takes less away from your past.

But these retroactive effects can only go so far. Even an early death can't stop you from having achieved the things you did achieve while alive, such as getting into the veterinary program and passing all its exams. It can't deprive you of the pleasures you felt, the understanding you had, or the kindly actions you performed—their value is undiminished. Though death can reduce the value of your past a little, its main harm is to deprive you of your future.

But this means there's a partial answer to death: to live as well as you can while you're alive, enjoying as many of life's goods as possible. If you do, then whatever its other effects, death can't reverse the fact that you did so. It will always be true, into eternity, that you understood those truths, accomplished those goals, and cared for those people. Yes, your life could have been better; you could have lived longer, and you could have done more in the time you had. But that doesn't detract from the goods your life did contain and always will have contained.

This is even more so given a major theme of this book. Some philosophers have held that there's one life that's best for everyone: the philosopher's (Plato, Aristotle), the life of virtue (the Stoics), the life of powerful willing (Nietzsche). This has sometimes meant that the best or even any good life can be lived only by a small minority with the specific talent for it; the rest can have only a much less valuable existence.

The rest then can't answer death in the way I've just described: they can't make it always true that they lived a significantly good life. But if there are many intrinsic goods and therefore many desirable lives, all or at least many of us *can* give that answer. We can select some good life from the large number of possible ones and make it ours. Though we can't stop death from depriving us of more good, we can make it eternally true that we lived a life containing some desirable selection of the best things in life.

FURTHER READINGS

Wilhelm von Humboldt's remarks about the value of well-roundedness are in *The Limits of State Action*, Marx's in *The German Ideology*, and Nietzsche's in *Thus Spake Zarathustra*, *Beyond Good and Evil*, and several other works. I discuss this value and the opposed factors of the dilettante's disadvantage and the costs of concentration in *Perfectionism*, chap. 7. The issue about calculating the overall good in your life parallels that of calculating the overall good in a human population, as discussed in pt. 4 of Derek Parfit's *Reasons and Persons*; I discuss summing, averaging, and the intermediate view that can object to some low-quality additions in chap. 6 of *Perfectionism*. Epicurus argues that death is not bad in his *Letter to Monoeceus*; the reply that dying can be bad because it deprives you of future goods is made by Thomas Nagel in "Death."

BIBLIOGRAPHY

Aquinas, St. Thomas. *Summa Theologica*. Translated by the Fathers of the English Dominican Province. 4 vols. Westminster, MD: Christian Classics, 1981.

Arendt, Hannah. *Eichmann in Jerusalem*. Harmondsworth: Penguin, 1963.

Aristotle. *Nicomachean Ethics*. Translated by W. D. Ross and J. O. Urmson. In *The Complete Works of Aristotle*. Edited by Jonathan Barnes. 2 vols. Princeton, NJ: Princeton University Press, 1984.

Bentham, Jeremy. *Introduction to the Principles of Morals and Legislation*. Edited by J. H. Burns and H. L. A. Hart. London: Methuen, 1970.

Broad, C. D. *Examination of McTaggart's Philosophy*. 2 vols. Cambridge: Cambridge University Press, 1933–38.

————. *Five Types of Ethical Theory*. London: Routledge and Kegan Paul, 1930.

Browning, Robert. *Poems of Robert Browning*. Edited by Donald Smalley. Boston: Houghton Mifflin, 1956.

Butler, Joseph. "Fifteen Sermons Preached at the Rolls Chapel." In *The Works of Bishop Butler*. Edited by J. H. Bernard. 2 vols. London: Macmillan, 1900.

Carritt, E. F. *The Theory of Morals*. London: Oxford University Press, 1928.

Csikszentmihalyi, Mihaly. *Flow: The Psychology of Optimal Experience*. New York: Harper and Row, 1990.

Descartes, René. *Meditations on First Philosophy*. In *The Philosophical Works of Descartes*. Translated by Elizabeth S. Haldane and G. R. T. Ross. 2 vols. Cambridge: Cambridge University Press, 1911.

Dickens, Charles. *A Tale of Two Cities*. Harmondsworth: Penguin, 1970.

Elster, Jon. *Sour Grapes: Studies in the Subversion of Rationality*. Cambridge: Cambridge University Press, 1983.

Epicurus. "Letter to Monoeceus." In *Hellenistic Philosophy: Introductory Readings*. Translated by Brad Inwood and L. P. Gerson. Indianapolis, IN: Hackett, 1988.

Feinberg, Joel. "Psychological Egoism." In *Moral Philosophy: Selected Readings*. 2nd edition. Edited by George Sher. Fort Worth, TX: Harcourt Brace, 1996.

Frank, Robert H. *Luxury Fever: Why Money Fails to Satisfy in an Era of Excess*. New York: Free Press, 1999.

Gardner, Howard. *Frames of Mind: The Theory of Multiple Intelligences*. New York: Basic Books, 1983.

Gilbert, Daniel. *Stumbling on Happiness*. New York: Alfred A. Knopf, 2006.

Green, T. H. *Prolegomena to Ethics*. Edited by A. C. Bradley. Oxford: Clarendon Press, 1883.

Haybron, Daniel M. *The Pursuit of Unhappiness: The Elusive Psychology of Well-Being*. Oxford: Oxford University Press, 2008.

Hegel, G. W. F. *Phenomenology of Spirit*. Translated by A. V. Miller. Oxford: Oxford University Press, 1977.

Hobbes, Thomas. *Leviathan*. Edited by C. B. Macpherson. Harmondsworth: Penguin, 1968.

Homer. *Odyssey*. Translated by E. V. Rieu. Baltimore: Penguin, 1946.

Horace. *Odes and Epodes*. Edited by T. E. Page. London: Macmillan, 1883.

Hurka, Thomas. "The Justification of National Partiality." In *The Morality of Nationalism*. Edited by Robert McKim and Jeff McMahan. New York: Oxford University Press, 1997.

———. *Perfectionism*. New York: Oxford University Press, 1993.

———. *Virtue, Vice, and Value*. New York: Oxford University Press, 2001.

Humboldt, Wilhelm von. *The Limits of State Action*. Translated by J. W. Burrow. Cambridge: Cambridge University Press, 1969.

Hume, David. *A Treatise of Human Nature*. Edited by L. A. Selby-Bigge. Oxford: Clarendon Press, 1888.

Huxley, Aldous. *Brave New World: A Novel*. London: Chatto and Windus, 1932.

Kant, Immanuel. *The Doctrine of Virtue: Part II of The Metaphysic of Morals*. Translated by Mary J. Gregor. Philadelphia: University of Pennsylvania Press, 1964.

———. *Groundwork of the Metaphysics of Morals*. Translated by Mary Gregor. Cambridge: Cambridge University Press, 1998.

———. "Occupation." In *Lectures on Ethics*. Translated by Louis Infield. London: Methuen, 1979.

Kundera, Milan. *The Unbearable Lightness of Being*. Translated by Michael Henry Heim. New York: Harper and Row, 1984.

Larkin, Philip. *Collected Poems*. Edited by Anthony Thwaite. London: Faber and Faber, 1988.

Layard, Richard. *Happiness: Lessons from a New Science*. New York: Penguin, 2005.

Lessing, Gotthold Ephraim. *Nathan der Weise*. Edited by E. H. Hutton. London: Macmillan, 1962.

Marx, Karl. *Karl Marx: Selected Writings*. Edited by David McLellan. Oxford: Oxford University Press, 1977.

Mayerfeld, Jamie. *Suffering and Moral Responsibility*. New York: Oxford University Press, 1999.

Mill, John Stuart. *Utilitarianism*. Edited by Roger Crisp. Oxford: Oxford University Press, 1998.

Moore, G. E. *Principia Ethica*. Cambridge: Cambridge University Press, 1903.

Nagel, Thomas. "Death." In *Mortal Questions*. Cambridge: Cambridge University Press, 1979.

Nettle, Daniel. *Happiness: The Science Behind Your Smile*. Oxford: Oxford University Press, 2005.

Newman, John Henry. *Certain Difficulties Felt by Anglicans in Catholic Teaching*. 2 vols. London: Longmans, 1900.

Nietzsche, Friedrich. *Beyond Good and Evil*. Translated by Walter Kaufmann. New York: Vintage, 1966.

———. *On the Genealogy of Morals*. Translated by Walter Kaufmann and R. J. Hollingdale. New York: Vintage, 1969.

———. *Thus Spake Zarathustra*. In *The Portable Nietzsche*. Edited by Walter Kaufmann. New York: Viking, 1954.

———. *The Will to Power*. Translated by Walter Kaufmann and R. J. Hollingdale. New York: Vintage, 1968.

Nozick, Robert. *Anarchy, State, and Utopia*. New York: Basic Books, 1974.

———. *The Examined Life: Philosophical Meditations*. New York: Simon and Schuster, 1989.

———. "On the Randian Argument." In *Socratic Puzzles*. Cambridge, MA: Harvard University Press, 1997.

Parfit, Derek. *Reasons and Persons*. Oxford: Clarendon Press, 1984.

Plato. "Apology." Translated by Hugh Tredennick. In *The Collected Dialogues of Plato*. Edited by Edith Hamilton and Huntington Cairns. Princeton, NJ: Bollingen, 1961.

———. *Republic*. Translated by Paul Shorey. In *The Collected Dialogues of Plato*. Edited by Edith Hamilton and Huntington Cairns. Princeton, NJ: Bollingen, 1961.

———. "Symposium." Translated by Michael Joyce. In *The Collected Dialogues of Plato*. Edited by Edith Hamilton and Huntington Cairns. Princeton, NJ: Bollingen, 1961.

Pope, Alexander. *Poetical Works*. Edited by Herbert Davis. London: Oxford University Press, 1966.

Popper, Karl R. *The Open Society and Its Enemies*. Princeton, NJ: Princeton University Press, 1950.

Rashdall, Hastings. *The Theory of Good and Evil*. 2 vols. London: Oxford University Press, 1907.

Ross, W. D. *The Right and the Good*. Oxford: Clarendon Press, 1930.

Seligman, Martin E. P. *Authentic Happiness*. New York: Free Press, 2002.

Shakespeare, William. *The Complete Works*. Edited by Alfred Harbage. Baltimore: Penguin, 1969.

Sidgwick, Henry. *The Methods of Ethics*. 7th ed. London: Macmillan, 1907.

Sober, Elliott, and David Sloan Wilson. *Unto Others: The Evolution and Psychology of Unselfish Behavior*. Cambridge, MA: Harvard University Press, 1998.

The Stoics Reader: Selected Writings and Testimonia. Translated by Brad Inwood and Lloyd P. Gerson. Indianapolis, IN: Hackett, 2008.

Stocker, Michael. "The Schizophrenia of Modern Ethical Theories." In *Virtue Ethics*. Edited by Roger Crisp and Michael Slote. Oxford: Oxford University Press, 1997.

Suits, Bernard. *The Grasshopper: Games, Life, and Utopia*. Toronto: University of Toronto Press, 1978; reprint: Peterborough, ON: Broadview Press, 2005.

Sumner, L. W. *Welfare, Happiness, and Ethics*. Oxford: Clarendon Press, 1996.

Velleman, J. David. "Love as a Moral Emotion." *Ethics* 109 (1999): 338–74.

Wilde, Oscar. *Lady Windermere's Fan*. Harmondsworth: Penguin, 2007.

INDEX